The *F*

"Nothing could be a more ⌐ ... ⌐ women are engaged in now, trying to co ... wer in a way that delivers us to our highest selves. Kudos to Amy Stanton and Catherine Connors for exploring issues—often hidden, sometimes painful—that pave the way to genuine deliverance from the forces that hold us back."

—Marianne Williamson

"I'd love for my daughter to grow up in a world where then men and women in her life support her and in which she won't have to sacrifice her femininity for the expense of her success. *The Feminine Revolution* is a beautiful exploration of that idea and can help lay the groundwork for that future."

—Justin Baldoni, actor, filmmaker, and public speaker

"This book is the invitation and the opportunity and permission for us to take back what we already know to be true, which is *femininity* is quite literally synonymous with *powerful.*"

—Alexis Jones, co-founder of I Am That Girl

"The new femininity cultivates a new terrain in mind, body, and spirit for women. It establishes a new linguistic abstraction and way of being that demonstrates the real power of qualities such as lovingness, collaboration, and compassion."

—Dr. Habib Sadeghi, author of *The Clarity Cleanse*

"We're in the middle of a revolution right now, a movement that we won't even understand how big until years down the road."

—Cat Cora

"[*The Feminine Revolution*] inspires us to question the clichés and expectations of femininity and open minds and hearts to respecting the value of all aspects of womanhood, and humanity."

—Gabrielle Reece, from the foreword

THE FEMININE REVOLUTION

21 WAYS TO IGNITE THE POWER
OF YOUR FEMININITY FOR A
BRIGHTER LIFE AND A BETTER WORLD

AMY STANTON & CATHERINE CONNORS

SEAL PRESS

Seal Press
1700 Fourth Street
Berkeley, California
www.sealpress.com

Printed in the United States of America

Published by Seal Press, an imprint of Perseus Books, LLC, a subsidiary of Hachette Book Group, Inc. The Seal Press name and logo is a trademark of the Hachette Book Group.

The Hachette Speakers Bureau provides a wide range of authors for speaking events. To find out more, go to www.hachettespeakersbureau.com or call (866) 376-6591.

The publisher is not responsible for websites (or their content) that are not owned by the publisher.

Cover design by Anna Dorfman.

Print book interior design by Trish Wilkinson.

Library of Congress Cataloging-in-Publication Data have been applied for.

ISBNs: 978-1-58005-812-4 (paperback); 978-1-58005-813-1 (e-book)

LSC-C

10 9 8 7 6 5 4 3 2

CONTENTS

FOREWORD

by Gabrielle Reece

I was fortunate enough to begin my young adult professional life as an athlete, a role in which I had the opportunity to embrace my physical and competitive side. It was sometimes a struggle, but from a pretty young age I did learn how to be assertive and even powerful at times. It still took me until my thirties to stop apologizing and trying to be less-than to make others feel good. Spending time with female athletes and coaches who encouraged me to be aggressive—a trait that's typically considered "masculine"—trained me to accept this part of my own nature, my unique expression of *femininity*. I realized that being strong and aggressive did not take away from or diminish my femininity.

Since my days of being a jock, I have become an entrepreneur, a wife (I am married to what one would call an "alpha male"), and the mother of three daughters. In each of these roles, I find myself connecting with my female identity. In every aspect of my life, as a woman and a human, I ask myself, How do I want to express myself? What do I want to stand for? What parts of my identity do I want to foster, even if others expect something different from me?

At a certain point I began to enjoy and cherish all aspects of my femininity, whether others value them or not. This is the dazzling message of *The Feminine Revolution*. In these pages, Amy Stanton and Catherine Connors call on women everywhere to defy the definition of feminine traits as "weak" or "frivolous" (and, likewise, to stop defining "strong" and "powerful" traits as primarily masculine). They encourage us all to rethink the way our culture has decided that feminine traits are unimportant, or superficial, or fragile, and to see them as powerful gifts. I already know this is true and have seen it manifest in my own life: My intuition guides me like a North Star. My respect for beauty honors the visual wonders of our bountiful world. My gentle kindness to others begets more kindness and makes our world a better place.

As I raise three daughters, my hope for them—and what *The Feminine Revolution* offers—is a larger more nuanced understanding of our authentic identities. It inspires us to question the clichés and expectations of femininity and open minds and hearts to respecting the value of all aspects of womanhood, and humanity. We all must create the space for ourselves to honor our inclinations and distance ourselves from the external noise that labels anything that feels natural to us as "less than" or "unimportant."

The Feminine Revolution has arrived at the perfect time. It is time, separately and together, for women to tap into the so-called feminine trait of *love*, the most powerful of them all. We will call on our culture to appreciate the multifaceted nature of femininity: whether we are nurturing, multitasking, displaying emotional intelligence, insisting on authority, or otherwise doing some real ass kicking, we are women and we claim these capabilities as strengths. We all have the opportunity to explore and celebrate the infinite sides of ourselves, and we will not apologize for who we are or what we offer the world.

I want my daughters and yours to make their voices fluid without fear of dismissal. I want them to foster their gifts and find beauty in what makes us all the same. Core values like love, hard work, and honesty will always be essential to the foundation of our lives, and from there, how we want to color our lives with individuality is the greatest discovery of all.

I thank Amy and Catherine for writing *The Feminine Revolution* and for encouraging us all to embark on that discovery. Here's to you—all of you—in good health and adventure.

Remember what it was to be me:
that is always the point.

—JOAN DIDION,
AMERICAN WRITER AND JOURNALIST

INTRODUCTION

We've been talking about femininity from the very first moment that we met. We were introduced by a mutual friend who knew that we shared an interest—a passion—for women's issues and for questions concerning femininity in particular. When we sat down for the first time, we fell immediately into a conversation that went on for hours.

Amy was grappling with the question of why we're so hard on our feminine selves. She had always struggled with her own personal journey of balancing her professional demeanor—strong, confident, in control—with her softer and more vulnerable personal side. She wondered if this was getting in the way of her finding a great guy and starting a family, which she wants so much. And she had seen a similar and consistent trend among her woman friends and colleagues. "Why do we tend to be so critical of femininity?" she asked. Why don't we more openly celebrate that part of ourselves? Catherine had some theories—as an executive at the Walt Disney Company responsible for women's digital content, she'd been struggling to reconcile the femininity of princesses with the fierceness of girl power. And she'd struggled with this question as an academic and as the mom of a daughter (and a son) who loved princesses. The "femininity" of princesses, like femininity in general, she suggested, was freighted with too many cultural assumptions. We can't see how powerful Cinderella's compassion is, she said, because we're conditioned to look at that feminine quality, or actions associated with it,

*I don't have a
gut reaction to
the concept of
femininity. It
would be like
asking what my
initial reaction
is to the concept
of height.
And to assign
it a positive
or negative
connotation is
to mark it as
either an asset or
an affliction—
neither of which
I believe it should
be. It's part of
who people are.*

—SELA WARD,
ACTRESS

as weak. Amy jumped on this: But why do we think of them as weak? And is it possible to reframe them as strong?

We talked for hours. And then we talked some more. We moved from theories and hypotheses to personal experience and realized that we had even more to draw from. We were both successful women in the prime of our lives—high achievers who had fought to realize our dreams—and yet we struggled to reconcile our femininity with the moves that we needed to make to maintain that success. We were princesses in our own fairy tales, successfully chasing our own happily ever afters—but we couldn't help feeling that we weren't quite getting it right. What if we wanted to just enjoy our ball gowns and glass slippers? Was that okay? Shouldn't we be donning armor and fighting dragons or something? Was it possible to fight our battles while not giving up our ball gowns?

We resolved to figure it out.

It hasn't always been straightforward. As is probably clear from our opening stories, the two of us have had very different experiences of femininity, and we came to our understanding of feminine power via very different paths. But we share this core conviction: regardless of what femininity means to you, and regardless of whether you consider it to be driven by nature or by nurture, it contains the seeds of what we believe are our greatest powers.

We also share this belief: exploring or exercising the power of femininity does not presuppose or require adopting any particular political position. Femininity is not the domain of conservative or religious women; nor is it—in its empowered form—the exclusive domain of liberals or progressives. Any conversation about power can very quickly become a political one—and to the extent that we believe that the exercise of feminine power can be transformative for women broadly, there's a politics to this conversation, too—but we don't think this discussion is restricted to any side of the political aisle. Nor should it be, if we believe that tapping into feminine power is a good thing that should be available to every girl, woman, and female-identifying person of any culture or creed. And we do believe that. Fervently.

Unquestionably, our upbringing—our parents, our environment, our role models, our family dynamics—has a huge impact on how we understand femininity. The women we have talked to have brought home consistently and clearly that our first feminine role models may have had the biggest impact:

> [It's important to look at] how women are raised, how family dynamics play into women's expectations and acting out of scenarios they have experienced, how fathers fit into the picture of shaping women's self-image, expectations, etc. And how mothers fit in. I see so many women who have self-image issues (weight issues, issues of desirability) because they have grown up not only in a culture but in families that struggle with this issue.
>
> —ELLEN TAYLOR, PhD

> How you grew up has everything to do with how you lean into your femininity and how well you appreciate it and respect it. So for me, as a black woman, femininity is always associated with being weak. You hear it all the time: strong black woman, black girl magic. There is an implied acceptance of strength without vulnerability.
>
> —CARI CHAMPION, SPORTSCENTER ANCHOR, ESPN

> My experience with my own femininity as an Indigenous woman is all about waking up every day with confidence. All that I do is done with confidence, from school to speaking engagements to modeling. Sometimes I reflect on the things I go through as a young Indigenous woman because it reminds me that not everyone's story is the same. We all have our own unique story even if we all came from similar backgrounds.
>
> —DAUNNETTE REYOME, MODEL

I cast women to be on my TV shows, in which instance they're trying to be very feminine, because they're always cast as the love interest of somebody else. They're never cast as just a female lead. It's almost always a male lead that they are the wife to, the ex-wife to, the mother of, the daughter of. So, usually if you're casting—if that's how you're looking at other women—you're hiring the woman to be feminine.

—AMY POWELL, PRESIDENT, PARAMOUNT TELEVISION

I say that
femininity is a
social construct,
and we [women]
are redefining
what femininity
is. We are no
longer the damsels
in distress. We are
leading Fortune
500 companies,
running for
president, and
we are in the
infantry, on
the front lines
of battlefields
marching,
fighting, and
bleeding like the
men standing
beside us. We are
no longer asking
for permission.
We are stepping
into our promise
and fulfilling our
potential.

—JENNIFER
CARROLL FOY,
DELEGATE,
VIRGINIA

I grew up during the wave of feminism in the 1970s. It was very empowering in most ways, but a kind of flawed strain of feminism took hold as well. In looking back, we ourselves failed to see the power in certain feminine attributes, subconsciously buying into the notion that feminine power is weak. We ended up suppressing the feminine in the name of feminism. And this then led to a terrible split; we sort of felt we could be smart and taken seriously, or loving and loveable but not taken seriously. It didn't feel like we could be both. Women walked around in these stupid power suits, for God's sakes—mimicking men in the name of female power! That split did not seem to occur as much in European women. European women didn't seem to think they had to choose between being powerful and being feminine and sexy. But a lot of American women felt we needed to make a choice; it was one or the other.

—MARIANNE WILLIAMSON,
SPIRITUAL TEACHER, AUTHOR, AND LECTURER

Others think that for some of us, femininity is part of our nature:

My daughter is so girly. In her preschool class she's by far the most girly. She's always in a tutu, she's only ever in pink. I didn't impose this on her. She picks her own clothes. Always has a hair accessory in, always has sparkly shoes. The extreme of any extreme feminine thing you could ever choose, she chooses. And, it's funny, because you observe when you drop them off at preschool, how every girl is so different. But I'm rarely wearing pink, I'm rarely wearing a skirt, ever, really. And yet, she chose to dress that way, whereas other [mothers] who are either in more feminine jobs, or don't work, maybe, seem much more feminine and their daughters might be a tomboy.

So, you realize how much of it is nature versus nurture. I'm also from a family of all girls. My whole life was femininity. That's all I ever knew.

—Amy Powell, president, Paramount Television

Our various conversations with diverse women had one common thread, however: many of us have been conditioned to believe that femininity is a weakness. We live in a world that privileges masculine stereotypes of power—a world that demands women adopt masculine behaviors to attain power and reject feminine "weakness" to keep it. And we've been trained—through our upbringing, through societal pressures, through cultural norms and values—to accept (and even embrace) this, to the extent that many of us become fully complicit in it: we adopt masculine behaviors; we convince ourselves that real power only comes through doing what men do; we encourage our daughters (and our sons!) to reject pink and tear down their dollhouses. Femininity, many of us tell ourselves, gets in the way of achieving real power. But is this really true?

We don't think so. And we think that most women would agree with us. We suspect that many women *want* to agree with us—we're all looking for ways to feel like our best selves, powerful and authentic. As author and medical practitioner Dr. Habib Sadeghi told us,

I see many of my female clients re-evaluating themselves in all the roles they play in their lives, from wife, mother, daughter and sister, to their professional relationships, as well. It's a significant shift in focus from being preoccupied with external influences like politics and the media that tend to dictate what femininity and a modern woman should be, to a more intuitive awakening to the kind of woman they want to be. For many, femininity as defined by their Baby Boomer mothers doesn't fit with who they are or how they want to

As I was doing my research for my TED talk and exploring the definitions of "femininity" and "feminine," I found that even in music, a musical note that's described as feminine is by definition a weaker note. It's literally ingrained in our culture, in our history, in our Google searches, and it's how we've been socialized. So while it's going to take a long time to rid ourselves of this thinking, we have to. Many of the "feminine" attributes by definition are actually qualities I find in myself that I consider the strongest.

—Justin Baldoni,
Actor

embody their feminine energy for their greatest good and the good of all those around them. The shift has placed a greater focus on how women embodying more of their feminine energy on their own terms doesn't just help women as a movement, but everyone overall. So for my clients, the new feminine awaking is less confrontational than decades ago and a more collaborative, holistic movement that knows it's an essential part (but not the only part) of a more cohesive society.

We want to own our power and to put it to meaningful work—in our lives and in the broader world. We want it to serve our personal happiness and the greater stock of happiness in the world around us.

So, why haven't we yet realized this?

In the last century, women have gained unprecedented (if insufficient!) power in politics and in the workplace, more independence and autonomy at home and in relationships, and, in general, more opportunities to excel and achieve. But this hasn't always resulted in increased happiness and satisfaction in their lives. In fact, some research suggests that women's happiness has been declining for decades. "The paradox of declining female happiness," as some have called it, points to the tension between the real gains that women have made over the last forty-five-plus years and, for some, a downturn in happiness.

One important reason for this is the persistent tension between women's dreams and aspirations and the real obstacles to their success. Despite all the advances we've made, we haven't even gotten close to overcoming gender disparities across all sectors: the wage gap persists; the leadership gap persists; we still have to fight for our reproductive freedom; we still face abuse and assault and worry about the same for our daughters. We haven't really broken the glass ceiling; we can't really have it all. When Beyoncé asks, "Who runs the world?" the real answer, unfortunately, is "Not us." Not yet.

But if real happiness—meaningful happiness—will only come when we close the gap between our dreams and what's possible, how do we accomplish that? More importantly, how do we manage it without losing ourselves in the process? We've been trying to close the gap for decades, but we haven't come as close as we need to—and we think that part of the problem has been that we've been trying to close the gap using someone else's playbook. We've been using the masculine playbook—the playbook that says be tough, be aggressive, take no prisoners, wear suits like armor. The playbook that says power only looks like brute strength and dominance. The playbook that asserts that femininity is incompatible with power—personal, political, or otherwise.

We say, let's ditch that playbook. Let's write our own.

Recognizing the real challenges women face in the quest for equal opportunity and self-determination, we think we need an approach that offers solutions that make it more possible for us to be our best, most secure and confident, and most authentic selves. Solutions that take *root* in femininity rather than reject it. We've been told for centuries—millennia—that our femininity holds us back, but we believe that it is actually a source of power. We believe that tackling the paradox of declining female happiness—and tackling the broader obstacles facing women and girls—requires starting a new conversation about the real force of women's feminine power and about what it would look like—in our own lives and in the world around us—if we fully understood, accepted, and unleashed that power.

But this is only secondarily a conversation about feminism and women's equality (although we, of course, believe that these are very closely related). We're feminists, loud and proud, and believe firmly that this is part of a crucial, broader conversation. But we don't want to start *this* conversation by talking about politics, policy, or ideology—other brilliant women are already covering that ground well (see our reading list for some examples). We want to begin a new conversation about femininity

Not all women express femininity the same way and quite frankly, I think all women have a different level of feminine energy within them. There are some women who I would say are a nine out of ten on the scale and then there are some women that are a two on the scale and I think that's equally beautiful and as long as they're able to express that facet to the degree that feels the most honest. It is about people having the courage to speak their truth and in whatever form that comes.

—ALEXIS JONES, COFOUNDER, I AM THAT GIRL

that starts with our unique gifts and the very real, very actionable power that resides within each one of us—in the practices, postures, and characteristics that we associate with femininity and that too often have been framed as the opposite of powerful. We want to talk about what it means and what it looks like for a woman—for anyone who identifies as a woman—to be powerful in her own feminine ways. We want to talk about why and how femininity is powerful and to make the case that leaning into one's authentic femininity is truly the key to success in our personal, professional, and creative lives.

And we want to be clear that we aren't talking about an external power—we're talking about the power we all hold within ourselves. This isn't the power that aims exclusively to "win" or to dominate others. This is the strength and confidence that come from connecting with our own special powers. It's about finding our feminine flow state, or what psychologist Mihaly Csikszentmihalyi has defined as "the optimal state of consciousness where we feel our best and perform our best." A state of ease and freedom, where there's no need to hold back. A state of living fully as our authentic feminine selves. Unapologetically.

Here's what we want to do: reframe the cultural assumptions surrounding femininity so that we can reclaim it as powerful. We want to evaluate and interrogate the social norms that have culturally defined what we think of as femininity and show how to reposition them as powerful. We want to rethink and reinvent femininity for girls and women and give them the tools to use it to their—our!—advantage. And, most importantly, we want for these revelations and this new way of thinking (and feeling) to inspire a new, healthier and happier, more feminine way of living.

And that's exactly what we're going to do.

We used to call girls like Catherine's daughter, Emilia, "tomboys." But that word is, arguably, problematic, because it implies that a girl (or woman, for that matter) who does not conform to girl-coded cultural stereotypes is not only not really a girl but somehow a kind of a boy. It tells girls (and boys, and women, and men) that there is a right way of being a girl and a wrong way of being a girl, and if you're the "wrong" kind of girl, then actually you're more of a boy. It also suggests to girls and women that certain kinds of power and strength are the exclusive domain of boys and men. Physicality, leadership, assertiveness, curiosity, inventiveness—these are culturally coded as masculine, and we reinforce that cultural coding when we characterize assertive, adventurous, strong girls as "tomboys."

And it goes far beyond the word "tomboy." We've arguably come a long way in terms of the cultural messages that we send to girls and women—advertising no longer targets women (solely) as housewives and mothers, for example, and girls see their strength celebrated in beauty-product commercials and underwear ads—but in some respects we've overshot our mark. The "strong" girl or woman is often characterized as tough or gritty in the masculine sense, or she's lauded for competing in a male field, or she's urged to disdain "girly" things like princesses or pink. The metric of success for girls and women, in other words, is how well they adapt to the standards established by and for men—to masculine standards rather than feminine ones.

Of course, we want girls and women to be able to move freely and equally in the spaces defined by men. But if that's the standard for our "empowerment," what does that really say about (what does it do to) femininity—the condition, characteristics, and posture of the feminine? When we tell girls and women—even in the most implicit ways—that power is masculine, aren't we also telling them that femininity is weak? What about the girls (and the boys!) who don't want to adopt masculine behaviors?

When we say that the future is female, do we *really* mean female? Or do we mean female bodies in masculine roles, behaving in masculine ways and asserting masculine models of power? Is that future only female in the most superficial sense?

> *There's no specific way to define femininity, it's however you find that makes you feel most at peace where you are.*
>
> —SARAH BROKAW, THERAPIST AND COACH

> *For me new feminine, in one word, is about choice. New feminine equals choice. If you want to wear lipstick and high heels, you can. If you want to wear sweats and sneakers, you can. If you want to be a stay-at-home mom, go for it. If you want to be a CEO of a company, do it. It's your choice.*
>
> —NICOLE EHRLICH, MUSIC INDUSTRY EXECUTIVE AND CEO, CAT CORA, INC.

Wouldn't a truly female future be a feminine one? If we're going to light the world with our ideas and our innovations and our leadership, shouldn't that power—that incredible, infinite, electric power—be feminine?

Of course it should be. Of course it *is*.

So, how do we do that? To start, we need to unpack all the baggage attached to our understanding of femininity. That takes some doing—it is, after all, a few thousand years' worth of baggage. As part of this, we must consider how that history has informed our understanding of where femininity fits with the biological experience of being a woman.

LOOKING BACK

As we'll see throughout the book, traits that are considered feminine—in the sense of being closely associated with women—have historically been treated as weaker or less valuable than those that are considered masculine. But as we'll also show, most, if not all, of those qualities have masculine analogs that are actually valued and considered powerful.

A closer look at the historical maligning of feminine characteristics and qualities shows us something interesting: nothing inherent to them makes them weak. It's their association with the condition of girlhood or womanhood that makes them problematic. If a man adopts those traits, they become powers.

We can see this most clearly when we look at feminine archetypes as portrayed throughout history in religion, literature, art, philosophy, and popular culture. Many of those stories cast women as weak, unpredictable, or unstable, but it doesn't take much of a twist of the lens for them to come into focus as stories of feminine strength. Consider Eve in the Garden of Eden: she's famously characterized as weak-willed and disobedient. She takes the fruit of the tree of knowledge of good and evil and shares it with Adam: woman gives in to temptation and then tempts man. But it's easy to read this somewhat differently: she takes the fruit, we're told, because it looks good—but also because she wants the wisdom it will give her. Eve understands the value of wisdom and wants it for herself. She is, in other words, curious, independent, and self-determining. Taken this way, we can go so far as to characterize her as the original disruptor—she literally (or figuratively, depending on your view of biblical lore) disrupted God's plans and became the catalyst for human development. A closer look at history, then, shows that femininity has always been powerful—it has just been repressed or misrepresented for most of social, cultural, and political history.

History also shows that cultural ideas about femininity don't really derive from biological sex assignment. Again, some (most) of the traits that we associate with femininity because they attach to traditional female roles become redefined as masculine (and powerful) when men adopt them. The power of the feminine, in this view, is relevant not only to anyone who identifies as female in body or spirit (biology or social history notwithstanding) but to human beings in general.

But if our powers are human and accessible and adaptable across sex and gender, why has the feminine been so derogated? This is a crucial question because that cultural and social history of maligning femininity has arguably informed our experience and understanding of femininity right up to present day. And it's our current experience and understanding of femininity that needs to change if we're going to reclaim femininity as the source of power that it really is.

The fast answer is that, for most of human history, women really have lived in a different sphere than men. Whether we're looking at the Bible or evolutionary history, men and women have led divided lives, with women in the domestic space, the space of home, hearth, and family, and men in the public space, the space of politics, leadership, and war. The ancient Romans even codified those distinctions and wove them into the very fabric of their understanding of morality. Public virtue was for men (hence the word "virtue" derives from the root *vir*, or

People have defined strong as not feminine, people have defined powerful as not emotional. Society has defined things that way. But that's not necessarily the definition of strength, right?

—CHRISTINE SIMMONS, PRESIDENT AND COO, LA SPARKS

When you talk to 100 women you get 100 different definitions of femininity but I bet they all connect to being able to show themselves. To having a voice and being heard.

—CINDY CRAWFORD, MODEL

"man," such that *virtu*, in Latin, means "manly"); the honor of women, on the other hand, was modesty (*pudicitia*), defined almost entirely by their ability and willingness to respect the bars of their gilded cage, the domain of the family, the private sphere.

These distinctions have stayed with us a long, long time. And we have imbued them with a power differential. We have associated the public sphere with more (hard) power, and so we correspondingly deem the activity of men in that space more powerful than the activity of women in the quieter, more reserved private sphere. Masculine activity, in other words, gets de facto treated as more powerful—and, conversely, feminine activity or traits get considered weak. Not because the activity or traits themselves are more or less powerful, but because we have assigned the gendered spaces in which they are practiced different values.

Why, then, do women not get treated the same as men when they move into masculine spaces, if the activities and traits in practice are the same? Well, because they're not men, and millennia of cultural conditioning have told us that the activities of the public sphere are masculine and so rightfully practiced by men. The same goes for men moving into feminine spaces, to some extent—stay-at-home dads still struggle against the idea that their presence in the home is outside the norm, if not outright transgressive. (If you know a stay-at-home dad, you know that he almost certainly has heard someone express surprise at his role—and that he has also almost certainly heard it characterized as "babysitting.")

And so women have struggled to adapt to masculine spaces by adopting more "masculine" behaviors. We've put on pantsuits and leaned in and proven that we can act in these spaces as effectively as men do. Of course, we're operating in more masculine ways: as all of our leadership role models for so many years were men, it makes sense that we learned to operate like them, thinking this would accelerate our rise to the top.

But it's worth asking: As "competing in a man's world" has moved women into behaving in more masculine ways, have we ended up devaluing our feminine ways? And if so, what impact has this had on our lives—and on our emotional well-being?

To put this another way, have we adopted "masculine" behaviors and character traits in a way that has moved us too far into the masculine? Once we start unraveling that question, a million others begin to emerge. How and why have we characterized certain traits as masculine and others as feminine—and valued the former or devalued the latter? Have we lost touch with unique qualities, feelings, and behaviors that connect us to our feminine selves? For example, when we devalue sensitivity—especially in environments like the workplace—do we disconnect from our emotional intelligence and powers of intuition? If we disconnect from the qualities that we identify as feminine because we believe them to be weak, are we disconnecting from one of our greatest power sources? As Dr. Habib Sadeghi asks, "Would anyone really suggest that the power of gravity is less important than the power of electricity?" Of course not. Which is why, he says, "the new feminine understands that feminine energy is just as powerful as masculine energy but in an entirely *different* way. . . . [T]he new feminine understands that you can be *for* women without being *against* men." And that is the work of this book: to make the case for being for women's power in a practicable way and to show how that power can be reclaimed.

But it's important to be clear: this book is not about being empowered (someone else providing us with or giving us permission to claim power)—it's about *actually* claiming our power and tapping into its sources. This is a conversation about the unique gifts, practices, and qualities that allow us to be powerful in our own authentically feminine way. This is about reconnecting with ourselves so we can connect in a more intimate and meaningful way with others.

Because here's the thing: femininity is powerful. It's really powerful. And being in that power doesn't only feel good and

To me, femininity is owning your personal power in a way that feels true to you. And embodying it in a way that embraces the parts of the ancestral women before you with the parts of your own female heart that need to be heard and experienced for moments ahead. All that and nightly bubble baths.

—SARA BORDO, CEO, WOMENRISING

To us Femininity means living in our own Truth as Women and embracing our beautiful uniqueness that our Divine created us to be.

—CHLOE AND HALLE BAILEY, RECORDING ARTISTS

lead to better relationships and a more fulfilling life—it can change the world.

LOOKING AHEAD

So, how are we going to show how powerful femininity is—and how are we going to show you how to use it?

The first piece is easy, mostly because we think that you probably already know—or suspect—that femininity really *is* powerful. Regardless of how you define femininity—as a particular set of traits and characteristics unique to women and girls, as culturally imposed expectations specific to women and girls, or as natural behavioral markers of the condition of being female (or all or none of these)—we think that it's pretty easy to spot the undercurrents (sometimes overcurrents) of power that run through it, especially once you're looking for them. Consider a trait like vulnerability, for example, historically considered feminine. We're all familiar with the trope of the vulnerable woman and with masculine insults about emotionality and vulnerability that derogate those as feminine ("stop being such a girl"). But we also know that embracing our vulnerability allows us to tap into a kind of superpowered self-awareness. As Brené Brown has so brilliantly shown, our vulnerability makes us human. So, we take a close look at the language and stereotypes historically used to define the feminine and then examine how those interpretations and uses of feminine language and feminine stereotypes have created barriers or held us back—all toward the end of showing how we can reclaim them as powerful.

Showing how feminine traits and behaviors are powerful is also our path to showing you how to use that power, because understanding your power is the first step to claiming it.

This, then, is the real work: digging into the language and tools that make this power possible. Words like "sensitive," "seductive," "emotional"—words historically used to describe women—have historically had their power turned against them.

These traditionally feminine words and attributes have been perceived variously as weak, manipulative, and shameful—as generally undesirable or even bad. With a closer look and a slight twist of the lens, however, these words become powerful. And they point to powerful practices.

The following chapters outline twenty-one practices of authentic feminine power (with a few bonus suggestions thrown in for fun!). Each chapter starts with a story about our own experiences in confronting a feminine quality or trait traditionally perceived as weak and then digs into the history, the contemporary assumptions, and—most importantly—the potential reframing of the quality or trait in question. So, in each chapter,

- we take a closer look at the history of this quality, examining how it's feminine and why it has been associated with weakness;
- we make the case for a fresh look at and a new approach to that feminine quality, reclaiming it as powerful; and
- we provide tools and ideas for how to implement the practice of integrating the feminine quality in your life.

Throughout the chapters, you'll read words of wisdom from a wide variety of amazing women, some famous, some not (yet!). Their voices bring unique and personal perspectives to each of the practices and an intimate look at the role femininity plays in their lives.

Not every practice may spark for you—some concepts will resonate more than others; some may not resonate at all—but, as we've already suggested, femininity is a unique and deeply personal experience. Your femininity probably looks very different from your best friend's femininity, or your mom's, or your neighbor's—and that's a good thing. Femininity isn't some predetermined, universal condition; nor is it a set of one-size-fits-all rules about "what it means to be a woman." Femininity is an experience that flexes and moves and evolves according to

The more successful I've gotten, and the more responsibility I have, the less feminine I feel.

—MELISSA PALMER, FOUNDER, OSEA SKINCARE

The idea of our value and our worth is so easily frittered away by looking to other people to tell you, are you powerful? You know, when you're in Los Angeles and you're over thirty and you're an actress, the next girl's coming up. So unless you get a new algorithm for value and sustainability, what kind of feminine energy can last you your lifetime? The kind that is constantly shifting and adapting to the new chapters.

—JENNIFER GREY, ACTRESS

I'm not sure why feminine and feminism and all these fem words have this bizarre connotation to them. It's like we haven't really outright owned them, and planted the flag for how powerful it can be. Obviously, that's hundreds of years of culture behind us, but I do think that there are so many different ways to express femininity.

—MALIA MILLS,
FASHION DESIGNER

In trans women's eyes, I see a wisdom that can only come from having to fight for your right to be recognized as female, a raw strength that only comes from unabashedly asserting your right to be feminine in an inhospitable world.

—JULIA SERANO,
WRITER

the terms of the person who is living and defining it. We hope that you will find the practices of femininity that suit you and, through this exploration, define your own experience of femininity and live it powerfully.

And that is what this book is really all about: igniting our authentic feminine power and directing it to the betterment of ourselves, our lives, our relationships, and our world.

AMY'S STORY

When I did my TEDx talk four years ago, I was nervous. Really, really nervous. I had been thinking about femininity and observing a real struggle in myself and others. I knew there was a conversation to be had. But putting together that speech was brutal. It felt like a scratch on the surface. And it was. Both because I knew there was so much more to say and mostly because I hadn't "figured it all out yet"—I'll come back to this point because it's an important one.

Through my own experiences and struggles over the years, and through conversations with hundreds of women, including friends, family, clients, employees, and anyone who would talk about it, I learned there was a deeper pain, a deeper issue, around authenticity and the freedom to be ourselves.

I could see my own through challenges at work—for example, instead of responding to challenges in a gentle and compassionate way, I would react. I would feel my adrenaline rush when I felt hurt or overlooked. Instead of using my gifts—like my sensitivity and communication skills—I would seem angry or frustrated. In relationships, I had similar issues. I would be hurt easily, critical, overly sensitive. I would beat myself up for being too emotional or too sensitive. I thought I was "too much." I had a desire to feel less, be less, and tone it all down.

Not possible, I later realized. And, in fact, definitely not the right approach.

For me, this journey around femininity has been and is about leaning into our true selves. Looking at our feminine (and sometimes overly emotional, moody, crying) selves in a new way. Giving ourselves a break, yes. And even celebrating these unique parts of ourselves that make us who we are.

While, yes, I have the capacity to be strong, tough, confident, assertive, I've learned to think about those qualities as supportive of the feminine me. Not instead of the feminine me.

And back to the figuring it all out part . . . I'm still figuring it all out! This is a journey. As my friend Sarah Brokaw says, "Research is me-search." Catherine and I invite you to be part of this new conversation to open channels and unleash a feminine power that the world needs more than ever.

> *I am an example of what is possible when girls from the very beginning of their lives are loved and nurtured by people around them. I was surrounded by extraordinary women in my life who taught me about quiet strength and dignity.*
>
> —MICHELLE OBAMA, FLOTUS

CATHERINE'S STORY

When she was nine years old, my daughter told me that she was a tomboy.

"What makes you say that?" I asked her.

"Because," she said, "I like a lot of things that boys like. I like basketball and motorcycles. I like surfing." She thought about that for a minute. "I mean, girls like surfing too and lots of sports. And I like other things that girls like, like dolls. But mostly I like things that boys like. And Story [her best friend] is a boy. So, I think I'm a tomboy."

"I wouldn't call you a tomboy, sweetie. I think that you're you. And you like a lot of different things, and they're not just 'boy things' or 'girl things,' they're things that you like."

"But you could call me a tomboy."

"But I wouldn't."

"But if you did—"

"I wouldn't. And I won't. I'll just keep calling you Emilia."

And that, I thought, was that. Conversation closed, no more talk of tomboys.

But then she asked me about it again, a few weeks later, after a friend (a girl) described her as a tomboy. And then a few weeks after that, she asked me what a "bad-ass" was. She had seen the word, underneath an Instagram photo of herself in dirt bike gear, on my phone. And then just a few days later still, she asked me whether Hillary Clinton was a tomboy. It wasn't until we were well into a months-long conversation about all of these things that I realized we weren't really talking about tomboys.

We were talking about femininity. We were talking about the complexity of femininity.

By most conventional standards, Emilia is absolutely what is often called a tomboy. She does like things that are culturally coded as "boy things." She likes sports; she likes adventure and action; she's all skinned knees and torn pants and messy hair. She surfs; she skateboards; she rides a dirt bike. There are some quote-unquote girl things that she likes—interfere with her American Girl dolls and she'll cut you—but she enjoys those "girl things" in a context that is, for lack of a proper term, "gender-complicated." Her favorite American Doll sits in a doll-sized wheelchair because "she hurt herself on her motorcycle." She wears her princess costumes with skate shoes and Buzz Lightyear wings. Taylor Swift concert stickers decorate the bottom of her skateboard. But she's no less a girl for being complicated. She's no less feminine for having varied interests and skills.

In fact, her femininity is a big part of what makes her complexity powerful. There's nothing "boy" about her power at all.

Her energy is powered by girl.

I think all the traits of femininity can be powerful when they are expressed in a way that unites and lifts rather than competes or criticizes. I couldn't lead a team or a film set unless I was able to be all of the things simultaneously. Expressing emotion that activates: powerful. Respecting others with politeness that unites: powerful. Leading with the intuition of an innovator with the heart of a caretaker: I've found that's where my power beats its loudest drum.

—SARA BORDO, CEO, WOMENRISING

In today's society, anything that is appealing to the eye is considered beautiful, including men and women, but what is the definition of beauty? What is your definition of beauty? In my culture the women are revered as the backbone of our tribe/nation. However, in my travels around the country, from Indian Country to the East Coast, I've come to realize that all women are the backbone of this world. Women keep the balance in their family. We are strong, resilient beings; we have to be in order to continue bringing new life to this world. We go through so much physically and emotionally yet still keep a smile on our face while crying on the inside. That to me is the definition of beauty. Now why do we still have to march for equal rights?

—DAUNNETTE REYOME,
SIXTEEN-YEAR-OLD MODEL AND ACTIVIST

CHAPTER 1

BE EMOTIONAL

I think women are amazing for being able to show what they feel. I admire women who do. I think it's a mistake when women cover their emotions to look tough. I say let's own who we are and use it as a strength.

—Gal Gadot, actress

"You're too emotional." "Stop being so sensitive." "Don't take things so hard." Most women have, at some point in their lives, been told that they're too emotionally sensitive. Even women who haven't been accused of oversensitivity have likely confronted the *expectation* of sensitivity: the assumption that, because we are female, we are more likely to respond emotionally in intense situations (or even not-so-intense situations!), that we like weepy novels and rom-coms and cry at weddings and baby showers and ASPCA commercials. Even if we don't ever react or respond in those ways, there's still an expectation that we might, or even that we should. There's a reason why Kleenex is marketed primarily to women.

This idea of women being emotionally sensitive is not new. Aristotle argued that women are more driven than men by senses and feelings. "Woman," he wrote, "is more compassionate than man, more easily moved to tears. . . . [S]he is more jealous, more querulous, more apt to scold and to strike." (Woman is also, he said, "less in need of nutriment." He clearly didn't anticipate the twenty-first-century

*Being easily
empathetic to
and responsive to
other people and
situations.*

—AMY POWELL,
PRESIDENT,
PARAMOUNT
TELEVISION

*Reading between
the emotional
lines—you FEEL
people more than
you "see" them.*

—ALEXIS JONES,
FOUNDER, I AM
THAT GIRL

*Having the
capacity to pay
attention, to
listen, to perceive,
to understand and
to acknowledge.*

—JENNA ELFMAN,
ACTRESS

*An awareness
and openness
to the present
moment and
what it is
revealing.*

—JILL WILLARD,
INTUITIVE

stereotype of women "eating their feelings.") The German philosopher Immanuel Kant, centuries later, argued that women were so driven by their senses as to be fundamentally irrational and, therefore, unable to commit to moral duty—basically that because they were only motivated by feelings, they were incapable of real morality. And the great French thinker Jean-Jacques Rousseau suggested that women made poor teachers precisely because they were too inclined to let their emotions rule over reason.

But what do we mean when we say that women are "sensitive"? The dictionary defines "sensitive" as "highly responsive or susceptible"; it derives from the Latin *sentire*, which means "to feel." It's closely associated with emotions: when we're not talking about physical sensitivity, we're usually talking about emotional sensitivity—that is, being highly responsive to emotional signals or influences, our own or those of others.

CATHERINE'S STORY

The first person who ever called me emotional in a disparaging way was a college professor. He was my first philosophy professor; I enjoyed his class, and I did pretty well in it. But he had a tendency to call more frequently on male students than on female students, and he seemed to affirm their contributions more enthusiastically—even when they just repeated what female students had already said. After one such incident—I had gritted my teeth as he praised a male student's brazen rehash of my own comments on Plato—I decided to discuss it with him. I went to his office hours after class and explained my discomfort with what had happened.

He bristled and denied it. "You're being too sensitive," he said. I blushed and tried to object. He put up his hand. "And you're too emotional. Come see me when you're ready to talk about philosophy." I was dismissed. I left his office and never went back. That whole conversation had disoriented me and made me doubt myself. Had I read something into nothing? Why had this bothered me so much? Why had I gotten emotional about it? Should I just toughen up?

Years later, I revisited the episode in conversation with a colleague, noting that I had, for a very long time, struggled to make sense of what had happened. "I think that he was an asshole because he was unhappy," I said. Disappointed in his academic career, perhaps, or discouraged about not having tenure. Maybe trouble at home. My sensitivity provoked him, pushed whatever button was most exposed, and caused him to lash out and shame me.

"You're probably right," my colleague said. "And you knew it even then. Which means, he was right, too. You were being sensitive. Just not in the way that he meant."

She'd nailed it. I had thought of my emotional sensitivity as the problem—the trigger for his reaction, the obstacle in the conversation—but it wasn't. My sensitivity had made it possible for me to notice a pattern and compelled me to address it. I had gotten emotional because it mattered—and because my emotions had tracked the pattern in the first place. I didn't get the problem solved, but because I had listened to my feelings, I did get to confront it and try to understand it. My professor had likely come away more frustrated and confused. My emotional sensitivity had given me an upper hand, even if I hadn't known it or made explicit use of it at the time.

That was the first time I started thinking of it as a superpower.

The development and navigation of the felt sense—our emotions and how we feel when we are experiencing life with all of its peaks and valleys. I believe it's linked to our instincts and intuition. I think sensitive means that you have specific feelings and strong feelings towards specific situations. And as a whole, you may feel your feelings on a deeper and wider level than an average person.

—Geeta Novotny, opera singer

Sensitivity is, of course, a characteristic shared by men and women, but there's no arguing that it has long been most closely associated with women and is usually understood as a feminine trait. Emotional sensitivity is arguably one of the most "feminized" human characteristics. Excessive emotional sensitivity was for a very long time (most of recorded human history, in fact) believed to be a physiological condition unique to women. The condition of "hysteria," which was for a long time strongly (although not exclusively) associated with extreme emotional instability, was a disorder of female reproductive organs: the word "hysteria," long used to describe excessive emotional disorder, comes from the Greek word *hystera*, which means "uterus." And even though "hysteria" is no longer used in medical diagnoses, we still have strong cultural associations between female reproductive cycles and emotional sensitivity. Pregnant and menstruating women are characterized as emotionally volatile: the stereotypes of the overly sensitive pregnant woman who cries at the drop of a teacup and the dangerously moody woman raging her way through "shark week" still pervade popular culture and stand-up comedy routines.

Susan Brownmiller, in her seminal book *Femininity*, points to the famous 1970 study by Inge Broverman and Donald Broverman as foundational in exposing the problematic association of traits like sensitivity and emotionality with a narrow understanding of femininity. The "landmark study," she writes,

> reported that "Cries very easily" was rated by a group of professional psychologists as a highly feminine trait. "Very emotional," "Very excitable in minor crises," and "Feelings easily hurt" were additional characteristics on the femininity scale. . . . As might be expected, masculinity was defined by opposing, sturdier values: "Very direct," "Very logical," "Can make decisions easily," "Never cries." The importance of Broverman and Broverman was not in nailing down a set of popular assumptions and conventional perceptions—masculine-feminine scales were well-established in the literature of psychology as a means of ascertaining normality and social adjustment—but in

the authors' observation that stereotypic femininity was a grossly negative assessment of the female sex.

The negativity associated with the assessments measured in the Broverman study—then and now—has real-life consequences. A February 2017 *Harvard Business Review* study found that potential investors are more likely to frame enthusiasm in female entrepreneurs as an emotional shortcoming. And researchers have found women's perceived emotionality in the workplace to be replete with "descriptive bias": because women in general are stereotyped as sensitive, their actions are consistently filtered through that lens—to their detriment. "Sensitive" female employees are less likely to be promoted to management than their tough, plainspoken male colleagues.

Men, of course, are rarely characterized as emotionally sensitive or emotionally expressive. Male heroes of fiction are seldom portrayed as tender or feeling: the tough hero resisting the expression of emotion is a mainstay of film and literature (there's a reason why Mr. Darcy—the emotionally closed male hero of Jane Austen's *Pride and Prejudice*—makes every top-ten list of desirable male characters and why that character made Colin Firth's career). Characterization of men as sensitive is often framed in a feminine context and, more often than not, played for laughs. The website TV Tropes—an online repository of cultural stereotypes that appear commonly in film and television—has a whole category called "In Touch with His Feminine Side," which outlines the category of male characters who "lack certain stereotypically male traits and may adopt some stereotypically girlish traits." Such characters "are sometimes referred to as being 'sensitive.'" The "sensitive man" in popular culture is "very open or in touch with his feelings and therefore appreciates things such as a good Chick Flick." Again, more often than not, he's the butt of a joke: the guy who can't get the girl because he's too much *like* a girl.

> *Emotion is a word that's really highly charged. We think of being emotional as being in hysterics, right? We think of the extremes of emotions instead of realizing that emotion is actually an intelligence, and that it's a way that we communicate, even without words. It's really valuable and very important.*
>
> —Dawn Cartwright, Tantric visionary

That said, there are exceptions—and the exceptions tell us something important about the real power of sensitivity. Male characters who balance strong masculinity with undercurrents of sensitivity are celebrated as complex and desirable: think of any movie character played by Ryan Gosling or Colin Firth. Their emotional responsiveness is a marker of their intelligence and awareness; sensitivity, in these cases, is presented as decidedly powerful. But there's nothing inherently masculine about that "empowered" sensitivity—powerfully sensitive female characters are rare, but they do exist. The blockbuster movie *Wonder Woman*, for example, takes feminine sensitivity to (literally) a superheroic level. The title character of that film derives much of her strength from her sensitivity—Wonder Woman is keenly attuned to the suffering of human beings, and her passion to defend them is rooted in this deep emotional attunement. Her strength, in other words, has as much to do with her emotional connectedness to others as it does with her supernatural physical powers.

Clearly, there's a case to be made that emotional sensitivity can be powerful.

Perceptiveness, empathy, intuition, "felt" experience—when we talk, as women, about sensitivity, we're often talking as much about a kind of experiential wisdom as we are about feelings. Sure, sensitivity is a kind of responsiveness to our own feelings and those of others, but think about what that responsiveness requires: it requires *understanding*. It's not blind reaction— it's *informed* reaction. The information just happens to come through our emotional senses.

Sensitivity is, in other words, actually grounded in knowledge—in our awareness and understanding of our own or others' feelings. It's wisdom based on experience: the sensitive person identifies and interprets a stimulus—emotional, physical, intellectual—as familiar and connects that stimulus to her own experience. She is, in other words, able to "read" her own and others' feelings—to process and respond to emotions and emotional experience more quickly and accurately than someone who lacks sensitivity.

This kind of sensitivity—sensitivity as finely tuned emotional intelligence—is characteristic of some of the most powerful female characters in fiction. The heroines of Jane Austen's novels—best sellers for two hundred years and many times translated into film—are, for example, models of sensitivity. Elizabeth Bennett, from Austen's *Pride and Prejudice*, is admired for her keen social intelligence and her disinclination to suffer unkind, insensitive people, including the seemingly unfeeling Mr. Darcy, whom she initially rebuffs (although later falls in love with, once she sees past his cold exterior). And Elinor Dashwood of Austen's *Sense and Sensibility* is deeply thoughtful and keenly attuned to the emotions behind the "polite lies" of other characters. These are conventionally feminine characters, and their sensitivity is characterized as typical of their sex—but it is framed as neither weak nor undesirable. On the contrary, it is a hallmark of their intelligence and grounds their appeal as characters.

And emotional sensitivity as a powerful, desirable quality in female characters is not just a hallmark of English parlor dramas. Powerfully sensitive women appear in superhero movies (the aforementioned *Wonder Woman*), television series (the titular character in *Buffy the Vampire Slayer* saved the world from vampires and monsters many times over—and understood their pain), and popular music (Beyoncé's "Sasha Fierce" stage persona draws from deep emotional wells to fuel an explicit fierceness). Even the much-criticized princesses of Disney's versions of classic fairy tales can be understood to embody emotional sensitivity in its more powerful form: Belle's sensitivity allows her to understand and sympathize with the Beast, after all. And what is Elsa—of the hit movie *Frozen*—but a queen whose sensitivity turns out to be a superpower?

Sensitivity *can* be a superpower, and all the more powerful to the extent that we appreciate and embrace its feminine aspects. Even if we don't assume emotional sensitivity to be biologically

I'm aware that men in very powerful positions always think we're emotional. They think we're more emotional and that's why we don't have more positions in leadership. They expect us to be emotional. So I'm aware of that when I'm talking to them.

—CARI CHAMPION, SPORTSCENTER ANCHOR, ESPN

*We have to
stop looking at
ourselves from
the outside in,
meaning through
everybody else's
lenses, and start
taking steps that
are generated
from truly how
we feel, to really
be in touch with,
How does that
make me feel?
Does it energize
me? Does it make
me angry? Does
it make me cry?
Does it make
me curious? We
say some things
are feminine
and some things
are masculine,
but it's really
this amazing
diversity of
emotion, and how
do we become
aware of what
triggers each
emotion in all
of us or doesn't
trigger it at all.*

—MALIA MILLS,
FASHION DESIGNER

or physiologically feminine, the feminine-coded idea of sensitivity as connected to our ability to empathize with and deeply understand the nuances of others' emotional experiences is a powerful one. It's considered feminine precisely because we've been socialized to think of emotional connection as the domain of women, and because we've been socialized to think that way, we have arguably been conditioned to cultivate and hone that capacity for connection. This is not to say that all women are or become perfectly sensitive beings with the capacity for deep emotional connection—but we are, most of us, pretty well trained in the art of emotional observation and the craft of cultivating connection.

And those skills—the skills of sensitivity—can and should be cultivated. Because they're more than just skills: they're superpowers.

Amy Powell, president of Paramount Television, points out that emotional sensitivity makes her a different kind of leader: "I'm more sensitive in meetings." And, she says, because of that she's always the person people go to if there's a problem. "I'm like the mother hen of the group in that way." We'll cover more of how being maternal can be a powerful leadership tactic in a later chapter, but it's worth noting here: being emotionally accessible is a powerful point of connection not just with our families and friends but with those we're trying to lead and inspire.

Of course, it's easier to be emotionally expressive if you're the president of your company. If you're just starting out in your career—or even if you're somewhere in the middle of it—you might worry that getting "easily upset in meetings" could work against you. That's a real concern, but it doesn't mean that you need to disconnect from your emotional sensitivity—you just need to know how to harness it.

Harnessing this power and tapping into this "new way of being" is easier than it might seem. Ask yourself, throughout your day, Am I paying emotional attention to the world around me? Notice what it feels like to pay emotional attention, in any given experience—to pay attention to your own emotional experience (the response of your emotional senses) and to the emotional experiences of others. Whether it's an argument with your spouse, a warm moment with a friend, or a tricky conversation with a colleague, pay close attention to how you're feeling, and ask yourself, What are my senses picking up on? What can I notice, emotionally, in this moment? If you pay attention, the social and emotional landscape around you will be as tangible and easy to "read" as the landscape that you can see with your eyes. What a power that is!

But your powers of emotional sensitivity are only as strong as you allow and believe them to be. And let's be frank—we still live in a world that attaches a lot of baggage to emotions and to emotional sensitivity, and so you're going to confront people, ideas, and social practices that will deny or ignore their power. Sometimes confronting or meeting that will be easy—you know that it's a superpower, after all!—and sometimes it will be pretty hard. But as you exercise that power throughout your daily life—in your work, in your relationships, and in your personal development—you'll deepen your relationship with your sensitive self, and your connection to your superpower will get stronger, as will the power itself.

So, *do* be emotional. *Do* be sensitive to your emotions and to the emotions of others. Your emotional sensitivity connects you to the world. It gives you insight into your own experiences and those of others. It is both a means (a tool and an ability that helps you get what you want) and an end in itself (the rich experience of being in tune with the world and with others is its own reward). Cultivate and enjoy it.

HOW TO BE POWERFULLY EMOTIONAL

Practice emotional reflection. Engage in "active noticing" of your emotional responses to stimuli. Seek out opportunities to have your emotional senses stimulated—through exposure to

The worst days for me are when I see women not supporting other women. It's almost worse coming from a woman than a man, to tell you you're emotional, or putting you in your place or not feeling like the light can shine on all of us.

—DEBORAH CURTIS, VICE PRESIDENT, ENTERTAINMENT MARKETING & PARTNERSHIPS, AMERICAN EXPRESS art and culture (music, film, books), through engagement with other people, through personal writing or other reflection—and pay attention to your emotional responses. What emotional stimuli are you most sensitive to? What do your different emotional responses feel like? How would you describe them? By paying attention to your sensitivity and looking for opportunities to develop and hone it, you're cultivating it as a power that you can use in all aspects of your life—and one that you can just enjoy for the rich connection and experience it provides.

Observe your emotional responses. Use your sensitivity to increase your situational awareness, build relationships, and boost your creativity. Leverage sensitivity in engaging with others; use sensitivity powers in managing both up and down. In meetings, use your sensitivity to stay attuned to what people are really saying and how they're really responding to each other: notice body language and social cues; watch for the emotion running beneath the surface of the interactions. Instead of leaning in and focusing on how much you're saying and whether you're getting attention, lean back a little, listen, and learn—and figure out how to use what you learn to your advantage. Maybe that go-getter at the end of the table doesn't really believe in the idea he's pitching; maybe your boss isn't as supportive of the ideas at the table as she seems. Don't just think before you speak—*feel* before you speak.

Remember that sharing your feelings is a cornerstone of good relationships. Use your emotional sensitivity to reach deeper levels of intimacy, to enhance shared emotional experience, and to improve communication. Again, don't just think before you speak—*feel* before you speak. Stay connected to your feelings when you're in communication with your loved ones— stay sensitive to the workings of not just your heart but theirs.

If you have kids, be an emotional parent. Use your powers of sensitivity to connect with your children emotionally and to model emotional awareness and responsiveness. Obviously you want to be careful about how you express and model anger and frustration—but remember that children do need to learn about those and that it's not only okay to feel those emotions but important to understand why and how they feel them.

Use emotions as a creative tool. Your powers of sensitivity can allow you to dig deeper into your own creative potential; leverage sensitivity to find your purpose and to connect that purpose to others.

For me, it's not so much about femininity but about embracing who you are, being true to yourself and being your best self. Being content with the female body you've been given and making the most of what you've got. Preparing yourself mentally and physically and being ready when an opportunity arises. I've never thought that power needs to wear a pantsuit. I'm in a rock band. The majority of the people I encounter on tour are men. I wear dresses on stage because it makes me feel good, not because it's what I should or shouldn't wear. It's what I like and it's personal to me. I don't want to fit in with the guys. I'm not thinking about how I can fit in. Power comes from within. If you're good at what you do, then it shouldn't matter what you're wearing. I think there is a decline in happiness because people are trying to achieve what others deem as ideal. You need to embrace your own journey, not someone else's. Love yourself, be the best you can be, be kind to others. Make the most of the life you've been given. Don't overthink things. Don't base your happiness on what others might be thinking. By loving and accepting yourself, you're embracing your femininity.

—NIKKI MONNINGER, BASSIST FOR
SILVERSUN PICKUPS AND MOM OF TWINS

CHAPTER 2

CRY OPENLY

Do not apologize for crying. Without this emotion, we are only robots.

—ELIZABETH GILBERT,
EAT, PRAY, LOVE

When we think about female emotionality, one stereotype emerges ahead of all the others: the tearful, weepy woman. A tendency to cry is regarded as an almost exclusively feminine characteristic—to the extent that even things that might provoke crying are considered feminine. Two-hanky movies, "weepers," books and songs that pull at the heartstrings: if it makes you cry, it was probably made with women in mind—or so we think, because we do associate tears with women. And even many of us who don't otherwise think of themselves as emotional will admit to being "criers" (Catherine: "This is totally me").

We think that women cry all the time—and in fact, it's been scientifically proven that women do cry more often than men. Or, to be more precise, men cry less often than women: research has shown testosterone to be an inhibitor of tears. And there are actually good, functional reasons for this: the same physiological processes that influence female fertility also influence tear production.

AMY'S STORY

I come from a family of criers. My family cries easily when things are happy, when things are sad, and everything in between. I've realized over the years that while these two things can go hand in hand, there's a difference between being sensitive and being a crier. Crying easily is its own wild beast. And for many years I perceived it as a challenge. Perhaps I didn't have the skills to calmly communicate my feelings, which meant that I'd get worked up, my face would turn bright red, and tears would begin streaming down my face. Even though it was normal in my family, crying always seemed extreme—I had been pushed too far. And I always regretted crying after the fact. I was ashamed of my vulnerability and sensitivity. I was embarrassed by the lack of control.

When I graduated from college and entered the workforce as an assistant account executive in advertising at a big advertising agency in New York City, suddenly the stakes seemed higher. Crying seemed less acceptable than ever. I think people have always been surprised by my crying and my supersensitive side because I come across as so strong and confident. Apparently in my case, these are the yin and the yang.

I cried my way through tough work situations, performance reviews, and embarrassing situations. I made people uncomfortable in some cases; in others, I grew closer to my colleagues as a result of their seeing the raw, vulnerable, real me.

While working with NYC2012, New York's Olympic bid, I worked for two strong, commanding, aggressive, and passionate men, Dan and Jay. They were and remain the mentors of all time for me. I recognized when we first started working together that they differed greatly in style from those I had worked for in advertising (Dan came from the finance world and Jay from politics and media). They were bold, brash, and, at times, yellers. And I loved it. After working for a number of catty, passive-aggressive women, I found their openness, transparency, and directness a welcome change.

But rest assured, I still cried. As foreign as their style was to me, mine was likely a surprise to them. The result? We got used to it and worked through it. They recognized my tears were a result of my fierce passion and endless care for our shared goal of bringing the Olympic Games to NYC. And that recognition and understanding led to a closeness and compassion that, I would argue, was not only powerful in our work relationship but also contributed to our closeness as human beings. They are still important figures in my life today (although I haven't cried to either of them in recent years, thankfully . . . but I could!).

These days I encourage my employees to cry. And sometimes they do (they're still embarrassed).

My office is almost completely women. I feel like they almost get to be more feminine than I do. Some of them cry, and I find myself, when they cry in meetings, being like, "Ugh. Why are you crying," because I don't get to cry.

—MELISSA PALMER, FOUNDER, OSEA SKINCARE

We all know that crying can be seen as a sign of weakness. Some of this is rooted in pretty basic facts about human behavior and social engagement: we cry when we're vulnerable or disempowered (because of age or circumstance) or to express emotion. In the absence of higher-order communication tools, babies and children cry frequently to communicate a basic need—that they're hungry or tired or scared or bored. Children also cry frequently because they haven't yet learned how to moderate their emotions: they simply don't know how not to cry. Thus we associate crying with vulnerability and immaturity. How many times have you heard someone say to an upset child, "Don't be a baby"? And how many times have you heard someone who is getting emotional be told, "Don't be such a girl"?

Crying is letting off steam. Some people go to a bar and get drunk, but having a little cry is much healthier. There's a big gender divide because I think men in general are uncomfortable with women crying. Because they want to fix it and it makes them very uncomfortable. I think it's a place where work needs to be done. We need better language. To be able to say, "Look, I'm a crier, you don't have to fix it but I've got to cry," and have it not be seen as a weakness.

—CINDY
CRAWFORD, MODEL

DID YOU KNOW? Studies have found that women cry, on average, over five times a month. Men? Not much more than once a month.[1]

Crying became associated with women and femininity not just because women do cry more but also because it is so closely connected to children and child-rearing. Women respond to and tend to tears, and children learn to moderate their tears through women (mothers, caregivers, and others). French Enlightenment philosopher Jean-Jacques Rousseau argued that the cultivation of emotion was the unique domain of women: mothers taught children how to feel deeply and to feel for and with each other. (This, for Rousseau, was crucial to boys' development as citizens—they needed to learn how to love their fellow man. Girls, of course, just needed to learn how to love.) Tears, of course, were a crucial part of deep feeling, but their expression was restricted to the household—the domain of women. Big boys—out in the world of work and politics—didn't cry.

This powerful gender coding persists to the present day. And not just for girls but for boys too. "How we're raised to adhere to cultural gender expectations plays a role" in how we understand crying, says Dr. Luann Brezindine. "Think of it as learning to play an instrument; you practice consistently and get better and better at that thing, and at control—little boys are always told to 'suck it up,' and little girls don't hear that. Boys are trained to control tears. They're trained to control their emotions. And if you practice that your entire childhood, by the time you become a young adult, you've gotten very good at it. Like an instrument, we learn to play the emotions acceding to our gender role."

ARE YOU CRYING? There's no crying! THERE'S NO CRYING IN BASEBALL!
—TOM HANKS AS JIMMY DUGAN, A LEAGUE OF THEIR OWN

We carry these biases in every aspect of our daily lives. We're conditioned to believe that tears in the workplace or in public are unseemly and immature, that crying in spaces outside the home makes us seem weak or out of control or shows we aren't equipped to handle difficult situations. But this also influences how we view private tears: we're so conditioned to believe that crying is weak that we often worry that even crying in the private presence of a loved one makes us seem needy, overly emotional, or even unstable. We're concerned that crying is a sign of weakness or that we can't handle our job. We worry that our tears will make people uncomfortable, and we worry about the repercussions of their discomfort.

Realistically, of course, crying will at times be seen as a sign of weakness—more times than we'd like. Sadly, that's just a fact of the culture we live in. It's also a fact that crying will make some people uncomfortable: bearing witness to the emotions of others requires power that not everybody has.

But so what? Are those reasons enough not to do it? There's a case to be made that alleviating pressure through crying leads to mental strength. Counterintuitive, perhaps, but as we explore our feminine power, we can take advantage of something that comes naturally to us, the gift of tears.

So, let's flip the script and imagine a world where crying is powerful. What if the physical and emotional benefits of crying make a case for why crying is actually a very good idea?

Let's start with the physical benefits of crying. Some research shows that the physical act of crying is actually good for us. It releases stress hormones. It activates the parasympathetic nervous system and restores balance in our bodies. We often feel better physically after we cry. Emotional tears (versus reflex tears caused by a poke to the eye or chopping onions) have specific health benefits. Dr. William Frey, biochemist and "tear expert," has argued that emotional tears contain stress hormones that are excreted from the body through crying and so do relieve stress.[2]

I lived half of my life thinking vulnerability, crying were weak things to do, which didn't make any sense. We're told vulnerability is weakness, and so people avoid it. But those who you meet who can own their tears and just say what they need to say—not in the way of the overshare and the, like, anyone who will listen please hear my problems, but in the way of powerful ownership of someone's own feelings and emotions as they're true to them in that moment. I am so drawn to that person.

—Emily Greener, cofounder, I Am That Girl

There is an ancient tribal proverb I once heard in India. It says that before we can see properly we must first shed our tears to clear the way.

—LIBBA BRAY,
THE SWEET FAR
THING

Often, the buildup to a good cry is an accumulation of stress, anger, pain, or fear—and the crying itself is a physical release of emotional tension. Of course it feels good to let all of that go. Why on earth would we want to keep this inside our bodies? Instead of avoiding and suppressing your urge to cry, what would happen if you let go and let the tears flow?

DID YOU KNOW? The Japanese recognize the healthy aspects of crying and in 2013 created "crying clubs," called *rui-katsu*, literally translated as "tear-seeking." According to the International Study on Adult Crying, of the thirty-seven nationalities polled, the Japanese are among the least likely to cry. (Americans, on the other hand, are among the most likely.)

Ad Vingerhoets, a clinical psychologist who focuses on stress and emotion, argued in his TEDx Amsterdam talk, "Tears have played an important role in our evolution and still do play an important function. Without tears, we as humans would never have become the empathic, ultra-social species that we currently are." He suggests that tears trigger social bonding and human connection. The ultimate vulnerability evinced by a good cry, in other words, allows people in, enables others to truly see us, and elicits empathy.

Others can learn a lot about you when you let them witness your tears. As Vingerhoets says, tears connect us with others: they communicate to others that we're sad or afraid or even just powerfully moved by something, which in turn allows others the opportunity to respond. Tears reveal our emotions—and so reveal *us*. And that's powerful.

Because what's more authentic than showing how you feel? Tears can be a sign of how much you care, how seriously you take someone or a situation, your passion for the issue at hand.

Rather than looking at your tears through a judgmental lens, what if you were to pat yourself on the back for being true and real and for really showing up in that moment? That's not an easy thing to do. Crying is exposure—the ultimate demonstration of vulnerability. What if you give yourself some credit for radical honesty and transparency about your own vulnerability? Wouldn't that be immensely powerful?

Crying can be a result of a bad day. A bad mood. A weak moment. A misunderstanding. It can be the result of anger, frustration, hurt, anxiety, or fear. So, instead of focusing on the fact that you're crying, try to focus on why you're crying. Look at the source of your tears: What emotion caused them? What do your tears tell you? How can you learn from what they're telling you?

HOW TO TAP INTO THE POWER OF CRYING

Don't hold back. At those moments when we feel we have some control (by the way, often we don't!), what if we let go? Take a deep breath, and whatever happens, happens.

Be vocal. Share your experience with the person you're crying to (e.g., "Is it OK for me to cry?" "I feel uncomfortable crying right now, but I can't help it," or "I care deeply about this").

Embrace the discomfort. Rather than avoiding those tough talks and uncomfortable situations, seek them out. Instead of running away from the tough conversation with a coworker or employee or from confronting your loved one about an upsetting topic, lean in. Recognize this is a source of power and growth.

Feel the freedom. Take a moment to assess the feelings around crying. Do you feel better after? Have you unloaded something? Can you put aside any feelings of embarrassment or shame so that you can benefit from these feelings?

Crying is one of the highest devotional songs. One who knows crying, knows spiritual practice. If you can cry with a pure heart, nothing else compares to such a prayer. Crying includes all the principles of Yoga.
—KRIPALVANANDJI, RENOWNED MASTER OF KUNDALINI YOGA

There is a sacredness in tears. They are not the mark of weakness, but of power. They speak more eloquently than ten thousand tongues. They are the messengers of overwhelming grief, of deep contrition, and of unspeakable love.
—WASHINGTON IRVING, NINETEENTH-CENTURY AMERICAN AUTHOR

Celebrating other women's strengths, it empowers you in a way, because it liberates you from comparison. You are going to do one or the other. You're never going to live in the middle, you're never going to be indifferent. People are not indifferent. Women, especially, are not indifferent. We are highly opinionated, so either I'm, like, "Wow, she kicks ass" or "Why are her shoes so high?" The sooner you can pick one, you're just liberated. Because there's always going to be someone great around you. It's just the way it is. Younger, prettier, wealthier, more athletic, more talented, more funny . . . whatever.

—GABBY REECE, ATHLETE,
AUTHOR, AND FITNESS PERSONALITY

CHAPTER 3

BE MOTHERING

Biology is the least of what makes someone a mother.

—OPRAH WINFREY, MEDIA PERSONALITY

Let's get this out of the way right up front: the act of mothering is in no way dependent on biology. Not just because—as we all know—many pathways to motherhood don't involve giving birth (shout-out to adoptive moms, stepmoms, foster moms, godmoms, and all the other moms out there for whom ovaries were not part of the process) but because "mothering" doesn't even need to involve children. Mothering is a type of caregiving that can be directed at pretty much any other living being. You can mother a pet or a friend in need—any person or being that you care for deeply and whose welfare you take seriously. To mother is to offer care and attention at the level of intimacy associated with family—it's to take meaningful, personal responsibility for the well-being of someone else. We think this feminine model of care is pretty powerful.

CATHERINE'S STORY

I was never one of those girls who played with dolls. Barbies were okay because I could pretend that Barbie was a spy or a superhero (she needed to be, to keep up with my Bionic

Woman action figure). But I found baby dolls and toy strollers distinctly uninteresting. Playacting at motherhood held no appeal because I just didn't aspire to be a mother. It seemed so dull, just taking care of other people all the time. Unless being a mother could involve international intrigue and daring adventures, I figured that it probably wasn't going to be for me.

I did end up becoming a mother, eventually. But even with a baby in my life, I still had a hard time thinking of myself as mom or mama or mommy. I love my baby, I'd think, but am I really a mom? Am I really able to mother?

It was a man, ironically, who set me straight.

A couple of months after I gave birth to my daughter, I brought her to the campus where I studied and taught to meet my colleagues and friends. When I went by the office of my dissertation advisor to say hello, we fell to chatting about studying and teaching and being a parent. "I'm a little ambivalent about all of it," I confessed. "It's hard to think about teaching when I still don't know how to be a mother." He nodded. And then he said, "You know, they're not all that different. So much so that you'll weigh them against each other: here, you're caring about other people's children. At home, you're caring about your own."

My mind, to put it mildly, was blown. I hadn't just started caregiving when I gave birth to my daughter. I'd been caregiving all along. I'd been nurturing—not with swaddles and bottles and lullabies but with ideas and books and dialog. I'd been tending to and caring deeply about minds and the hearts attached to them.

Taking care of others, it turns out, isn't dull at all.

Nurturing and caregiving are arguably among the traits most associated with femininity—in large part because they're so closely associated with the biological condition of being female. We link femininity with fecundity and fertility, with childbirth and child-rearing, and we tie caregiving and nurturing directly to these to the extent that they sometimes seem inextricable. What is nurture if not maternal love and care, or something very close to it? And what greater expression of biological femininity than bearing and raising children? The Madonna with Child is an archetypal artistic representation of femininity for good reason: the caregiver is feminine because it is feminine to be a caregiver.

But anyone who's ever known (or been) a caring friend or nurturing mentor knows that caregiving and nurturing aren't inherently biological. Caring and caregiving are powerful impulses—and powerful forces—regardless of whether the object of care is one's own child, someone else's child, or someone or something entirely other than a child. To "mother" someone or something doesn't require ovaries; one need only provide the very highest and most intimate standard of care—care at the level of giving or preserving life. And you don't need to have pushed anyone through a birth canal to do it.

But the act of mothering—and by extension caregiving in general—often meets with disdain and condescension. It's associated with fussing and overprotectiveness, with excessive caregiving. To be mothered is not simply to be loved or cared for—it's to be infantilized. And to be a mother is to be narrowly defined by one's caregiving; the work of mothers is too often reduced to very basic nurture-care and child minding, the sort of work that is basely physical, even animal. To say that a woman has "gone mama bear" is to suggest that she's surrendered to her basest animal impulses: her instinct to protect her young is so great that it can turn her, almost literally, into a beast. (Sounds pretty powerful!)

That impulse to care becomes all the more powerful in a context that's not so biologically limited. Human beings care for more than just their young—they care for their old, as well as their friends and lovers, their employees and clients, and their

When I had my daughter, I found that I became so much closer and so much more reverent and so much more inspired by women because going through that journey, you can feel alone in it, but also once you open up and you have so much humility . . . because being a mother, you have so many triumphs and failures every day. You feel like a failure and then you feel like a queen the next minute. And I think that encapsulates the feminine.

—GEETA NOVOTNY, WORLD-CLASS OPERA SINGER AND SINGING INSTRUCTOR

pets and other creatures. And caring isn't just a matter of tending to basic needs—we demonstrate care in tending a whole range of needs and desires, physical and emotional and intellectual. Teaching, too, can be understood as an act of care—no less so if Socrates does it than if a kindergarten teacher does it. The same can be said for mentoring, coaching, and any other relationship involving careful tending of and concern for another's development and well-being. These are mindful practices of care. Mothering can—should—be understood in the same way: as a powerful posture and action that, when exercised well, yields untold good.

It's also a passionate practice of care: the term "mama bear" can signify not just instinct but heart. A mama bear is fierce in the protection of her young because she puts the force of her whole self into it—driven by something greater than selfishness or self-preservation, she becomes capable of extraordinary action. We call a woman a mama bear when she exceeds our expectations of what she's capable of in caring for her children—and we understand that she's able to do this because of maternal love.

This kind of active, even ferocious loyalty and care is not, of course, exclusively the domain of women and mothers. Loyalty and the drive to protect have long been associated with men as well, in particular warriors and soldiers, who protect home and country and whose loyalty and protectiveness have been celebrated as acts of love (of a sort) since the beginning of human history. Philosophers have been making the connection between the force of maternal love and the courage of warriors for millennia. Women were considered ill-suited for war not because of their inferior strength but because their own warrior spirit would rise in defense of their children before their fellow citizens. Men could be trusted to love country over family; women could not. (Jean-Jacques Rousseau tells the story of the Spartan mother who defies expectation and celebrates when her sons fall in battle in defense of Sparta: "That," he says, "was a citizen." For him, she's the remarkable exception that proves the rule.)

We see this at work in the ways that we already express our mama bear powers, even when we're not mothers (biological or otherwise) or when we're exercising our power outside the family. TV executive Amy Powell says that she has been as maternal in the workplace as in the home:

> Every person who works for me somehow ends up being my child. I end up finding them other jobs, or helping them through a medical crisis. But you end up empowering [them]. . . . You become den mother for every single one. Which is like, in my case, 120 people, you know? But they come and knock on your door and share things that . . . like, one person is having an IVF transfer tomorrow, you know? Just random things that they would never say that to their male boss, ever, for sure. And also, I empower them a lot, and I'm also more generous with things like, "take as much time as you need, obviously," or I would never ask them when they're coming back. When I had my babies, everyone was like, "When are you coming back?" That was the first word, before congratulations. But I think that when women behave not nicely to each other in the work place, it often is more masculine qualities that they're bringing out.

To care and tend and protect at the level of a mother is pretty remarkable—that is to say, very powerful. How can you do more of this in your life—regardless of whether you have children? Ask yourself, Who needs my care today? Remember that mama bears are also warriors: they have the capacity to love and care beyond their home. Defend someone at work. Buy a stranger a coffee. Make your partner his or her favorite meal. Send your mom flowers.

Imagine if we were all mama bears to each other, always.

I feel my most feminine when I'm at home taking care of my family, when I'm giving, when I'm mothering or when I'm doing for other people. That's where I feel the most connected to the feminine in myself.

—CINDY CRAWFORD, MODEL

Whether it's being a mom, or in your job too, when you see your team grow and succeed, when you see them have such incredible success, those moments are the moments also where you feel innately proud, protective, wanting to create even more levels of motivation.

—DEBORAH CURTIS, VICE PRESIDENT, ENTERTAINMENT MARKETING & PARTNERSHIPS, AMERICAN EXPRESS

We have to create a culture of care. We have been working in cultures of rigidity. But what does care mean? The best leaders in my opinion today are caregivers, not females, caregivers. A caregiver is someone that nurtures their [team's] talent, rises them to the top, inspires the best kind of work ethic with values, and morality, and purpose, and passion.

—Shelley Zalis, The Female Quotient

You are stronger than you believe. You have greater powers than you know.

—Hippolyta to Diana of Themiscyra, Wonder Woman

Let go of the idea that taking care of others is somehow weak or submissive. A mother doesn't submit to her children (at least, she shouldn't); she guides and supports them. Caregiving isn't service; it's a kind of leadership. Ask yourself, when caring for others, how your practices of care are modeling and enacting leadership. Make this a mantra: "When I care, I lead; when I lead, I care."

Recognize that mothering is part of your daily life. Regardless of whether you have children, you may be a mama bear. This is really just caregiving—paying active attention to the needs of others. And that's as easy as offering to order a friend an Uber after a dinner out or warming up soup for your sniffly spouse. Caregiving is an act of the mind, an ongoing exercise of evaluation and analysis. (What does my child/student/pet/orchid need? What is going to best further his/her/its development? How is he/she/it different from my other child/student/pet/fern? How do I adapt my care to his/her/its needs and best interests?)

Remember that caregiving starts with taking care of yourself. The mama bear can't tend her cubs if she's starving or exhausted. (Airplane rule of caregiving: put the oxygen mask on yourself first!)

The Course of Miracles is very feminine in feel, teaching that defenselessness is our safety and power. Defenselessness means openness to this emotional reality of this moment; it involves a certain kind of vulnerability, an awareness that I've given you the power to hurt me. But you come to realize that being vulnerable is the only true invulnerability; you trust not that the other person will always act as you might want them to act, but that you will know how to respond from your power no matter what. And, in that sense no one can hurt you. That's why commitment is so important. If we don't feel we can be vulnerable with someone, then we simply shouldn't be there. Being invulnerable to a lot of people is not the way; being vulnerable to someone who has earned your trust, that's the way of the divine feminine. When a woman is vulnerable to a man who did nothing to earn that trust, she ends up devastated. But a woman who doesn't even know how to be vulnerable is inhabiting the psychic space of the masculine, and that makes her a failure with men because a straight man is looking for a woman! It's been a terrible trap for many, many women.

—MARIANNE WILLIAMSON,
SPIRITUAL TEACHER, AUTHOR, AND LECTURER

CHAPTER 4

BE CHATTY

Gossip. The more you talk about why people do things, the more ideas you have about how the world works.

—JANE SMILEY,
AMERICAN NOVELIST

It's been said that women speak 20,000 words a day to men's 7,000. This data point usually doesn't surprise people—talkativeness, chattiness, and a propensity for gossip are all commonly thought of as feminine traits. The thing is, though, that's wrong. Women don't actually talk more than men do—the two speak roughly the same number of words per day. And if you look at cultural representations of speech, it's actually the other way around.[1] When you consider film, television, politics, publishing, and the workplace, it becomes very clear that we actually hear men talking much more than women. We're so accustomed to the idea that women talk more than men that we've long overlooked both that we simply don't talk more and that we hear men's voices far more often than we do our own.

So, why is chattiness considered a feminine trait? Well, consider the term "chatty." It doesn't refer to serious speech or public speech. When we describe someone as "chatty" or "talkative," we're not saying that this person speaks frequently or even well. The gregarious Bill Clinton had a way with words, but he was described as charismatic and silver-tongued. No one would have called him "chatty."

AMY'S STORY

In my twenties in New York City, I had a group of girl-friends who met for dinner regularly. I loved the ritual and consistency of our time together. We had a lot of history and always had lots to talk about. Specifically, lots to gossip about. We would debrief on everything going on in our lives—jobs, dating, surviving the grind of NYC. It was a great feeling knowing we had a community, particularly because my family was far away on the other coast.

Maybe it was our age, maybe it was this group's dynamic and history, but after a while it occurred to me that I was leaving these dinners with a pit in my stomach—an uncomfortable feeling about the various stories told and the people discussed. I knew that I could just as easily be the one talked about if I hadn't been there. Nobody's perfect, but I realized I was participating in and contributing to the not-so-nice form of gossip, or talking behind people's backs. I felt guilty. This wasn't the person I want to be. I knew I could do better. And that's when I decided not to do it anymore. From that point on, I'd still see these friends but maybe not as often and, more often than not, individually versus as a group. To this day, I adore these women—they're wonderful human beings and, as we've grown up (to whatever degree we have!), we no longer have these not-so-nice conversations.

For a period after that realization, I paid closer attention to all of my conversations with and about people. I would make sure that if we were talking about another person, it was because we were trying to solve a personal problem or help him or her in some way, not just for the sake of it. I still practice this to this day. I'm aware of the times I say something not so nice about someone and will often try to correct it.

> Above all, I've learned that communicating meaningfully with others to work through things brings us closer and truly does help us sort things out. We can't underestimate the importance of this kind of communication and this type of closeness. We as women are uniquely gifted with the ability to understand each other deeply, in a way that allows us to support and assist our loved ones.

We use terms like "chatty" and "talkative" to refer to a kind of superficial, lightweight speech ordinarily conducted within the confines of the private sphere. It happens at kitchen tables, over cups of coffee, or on front porches. It's chatter and light conversation. It is, sometimes, gossip, albeit not the gossip of TMZ or the tabloids: it's shared stories about life in community. It's moms offering tips about babysitters, neighbors worrying about how a mutual friend is coping with divorce, girlfriends comparing dating stories. It's the visual trope of the teenage girl lounging with a phone or housewives huddled over the kitchen table, gossiping over coffee. It's social talk, and although it's easily—and often—dismissed as frivolous, it's the glue that keeps families, friends, and communities together.

More than that, it is arguably the behavior that most makes us human. When Aristotle said, famously, that man is a political animal, he meant that human beings are social. And we are uniquely social, in a way that distinguishes us from other social animals, like birds and bees, in that we do more than just communicate with each other. That is, we do more than just signal and share information through sounds and symbols. We talk. We converse. We make meaning together. Sometimes we make meaning around significant things—the nature of justice, for example (Aristotle's favorite example). But mostly we make meaning— we create shared meaning—around the material of our everyday lives. That's how we build, extend, and preserve community:

It's just this kind of emotional investment in others that gives women the unique ability to be the master of their relationships, as women are by nature, relational. It's been said that people will soon forget what you said and did, but they will never forget how you made them feel. Women have a much better ability to instantly engage with the spirit of another person and in a genuine, not manipulative way, draw people to them and consciously create the kinds of relationships, jobs and life experiences they desire.

—Dr. Habib Sadeghi, cofounder of Be Hive of Healing

through casual conversation and the exchange of opinions and ideas—from superficial thoughts about whether the local bakery overcharges for its bagels or the neighbor isn't picking up after his dog to deeper personal secrets and social observations.

This kind of conversation, long characterized as feminine and sometimes called gossip, gets a bad rap—in part *because* it is represented as feminine. But gossip is actually a very nuanced and productive mode of conversation that women use in unique ways. Deborah Jones characterizes gossip as a language of solidarity between women—it is, she says, how women establish social reciprocity.[2] And sociolinguist Deborah Tannen argues that women establish rapport with each other by "telling secrets," which serves as "a way of establishing connections and negotiating relationships."[3] She distinguishes gossip that involves "talking against" others from gossip that involves "talking about" others. In the first case, the speaker tries to establish rapport in a way that potentially damages the relationship between, or alienates, those in the conversation and the people who are its subject; in so doing, the speaker undermines community. The second kind of gossip is different: "talking about" gossip aims to keep people up to date about others in a network of relationships and to establish social rapport based on shared concern or interest in the lives of other members of the community. It, unlike the first kind of gossip, is not only healthy but necessary to community bonding.

DID YOU KNOW? The noun "gossip" derives from the Old English *godsibb*, or "god sibling," the godparent of one's child and, therefore, one's intimate friend. Hence the close association with women.

We connect through "social talk," or gossip. It's how we learn about each other, how we establish and deepen our shared languages and better understand ourselves as part of larger social ecosystems. We bond and form community by sharing what we know of each other. It's also how we learn about ourselves. The idea that we learn about ourselves by thinking deep thoughts under oak trees or earnestly studying philosophic tomes in cafés or reclining on a therapist's couch is a mistaken cultural trope. We shape our ideas through social talk. (Aristotle's teacher, Socrates, knew this better than anyone. He was probably history's greatest chatter, having invented the very idea of dialog as a philosophic practice.) We refine our own ideas and opinions by sharing and comparing them. Philosopher Julian Baggini has pointed out that social talk involves "moral appraisal of other people"—that is, "it's about the judgement of what people are doing and whether it's right or wrong, good or bad." Like it or not, human beings have shaped their understanding of morality through this kind of shared appraisal. We would not have a shared understanding of the idea of justice, for example, if we did not engage in intimate conversation about how we understand justice and who in our communities is or is not just. (To understand how this works in daily life, consider how young children learn about abstract concepts like justice, fairness, kindness, and the like. They develop their understanding of these concepts by discussing and interrogating them in intimate social exchanges and by parsing social information about each other. A five-year-old's tea party is arguably a better place to learn about the finer nuances of fairness than is the university lecture hall.)

DID YOU KNOW? Some scholars argue that storytelling itself is rooted in the human practice of gossip and really took shape when we invented fire. Although we had already used gossip to shape early community, only once we had fires to gather around at night did gossip become more leisurely and move beyond the work of community to the social life of the community and thence to weaving stories about the history and beliefs of the community.

Intimacy is key to understanding why social talk is so closely associated with the feminine and such an important aspect of feminine power. Women's propensity for forging connection through intimate conversation is the very glue of community, social bonding, and the creation of social meaning.

That's pretty powerful stuff.

HOW TO USE SOCIAL TALK FOR GOOD

Practice small talk. Yes, even if you're an introvert. "Small talk" doesn't have to mean talking to anyone about anything; it can just mean light social conversation with people you care about, the kind of conversation that doesn't necessarily have a point but forges intimacy just because it signals that you're comfortable enough with the other person or people to just chat.

Be conscious of the difference between "talking about" and "talking against." Does the story you're about to tell help or hurt the person it's about? Does it facilitate closer social bonds between everyone in the conversation—including its subject—or does it fracture bonds for anyone? Consider this to apply even in conversations where you don't know the person being talked about. Use the old schoolyard rule: Would you want people to be having this kind of conversation about you?

Remember that social talk is a kind of storytelling. Constructive social talk can be a kind of art and so is worth practicing. Being a good social storyteller can serve you well in many sectors—making you a sought-after dinner guest or a great date or helping you knock business presentations out of the park. So, be a student of storytelling. Pay attention to the patterns and cadences of story in all of its forms. Look for storytelling role models: Is there someone you know—or a stand-up comic, TED speaker, or other public person—who you think really has a way with a good story? Watch and listen. How does he or she use story beats and description to make the story sing? Adopt some of these practices into your own social stories.

Pay close attention to the details. It's attention to and interest in each other's stories that brings people together, bonding them to each other. You have to care about other people to remember details about them and to engage narratively with those details. You know how great it feels when someone you've met once remembers your name—or, better, that you love Patsy Cline and think raisins in cookies are evil? That's because you've learned that he or she cared enough to remember the details. Being present and in the moment will help you remember these details that make all the difference.

I think femininity historically has been thought of as being only one-sided: only soft and nurturing and sensual and all of those incredible qualities that are definitely part of what it means to be a woman. But then all of the other aspects of strength and empowerment and voice and power and so many other attributes—I think those have been pigeonholed as more masculine traits. And I think we don't need to be so segregated in how we think of feminine and masculine. I think feminine can embody all of those traits—either equally or maybe some women have more of those traits than others. I read this interesting term recently, *gender-full*. These thoughts about gender and what is gender, it's not quite androgyny—it's more of an acceptance and an open-mindedness and awareness that we can within us have all of these attributes and hold space for them simultaneously and not hold them back. Because I think growing up as a girl, growing into womanhood, because of everything that is showed to us in the media, we are getting messaging and we're internalizing that messaging. And the messaging has been very one-sided for a very long time. And I think this whole idea of the new femininity is really challenging what that means. That part of ourselves that maybe we have put under the table or pushed back into the shadows— we're unleashing all of that and saying, "This is the whole me and it includes the strength and the power and the voice." There isn't one specific definition I have of being feminine—it's an integration of how we typically think of femininity and masculinity, but it's a full integration of all of those attributes.

—SHEL PINK, FOUNDER, SpaRitual

CHAPTER 5

OWN YOUR INTUITION

Practice listening to your intuition, your inner voice; ask questions; be curious; see what you see; hear what you hear; and then act upon what you know to be true. These intuitive powers were given to your soul at birth.

—CLARISSA PINKOLA ESTÉS,
*WOMEN WHO RUN WITH THE WOLVES:
MYTHS AND STORIES OF THE WILD WOMAN ARCHETYPE*

You might have a woman in your life—a friend, a family member—who you think of as possessing almost supernatural powers of intuition. Maybe you're that woman to your friends and family: the one they come to when they want help figuring out a path forward or understanding something they're going through. It almost feels like magic—we might call it "witchy"—the ability to understand, explain, see, or anticipate things beyond the scope of what most other people can do. But is it magic? And if it is, how do we get more of it?

CATHERINE'S STORY

I was raised in the hippie-dense wilds of British Columbia, so I've never been a stranger to alternative spiritualities and crystal-gazing woo. And I've always been a dreamer and so have always been open to the possibilities of magic and wonder. But I always held a pretty conservative—if arbitrary—line on what counted as magic. And I always had a bit of an aversion (probably because of, rather than despite, my hippie Catholic upbringing) to what I thought were the sillier varieties of woo. The kind that involved sage and essential oils. Crystals. Aura reading. Etc.

So, when my husband suggested to me, during a particularly stressful period in my life, that I go see a "soul work" specialist, I recoiled. Was he serious? Didn't he know me? Was he high? (He wasn't high.) I didn't even like therapists, never mind "soul work" therapists. I didn't care if he dabbled in it—whatever works, buddy—but I was just not that person. I was not a person who could—or would—have her soul worked on. I used to teach philosophy. And what even was soul work, anyway?

"She's an intuitive," Kyle said. "She just talks you through things and because she's so intuitive, she just really draws stuff out. Just try it. If you hate it, you don't have to go back."

"Are there crystals?"

"You can ignore those."

We had variations of this conversation for months. But my stress was just getting worse—I was trying to figure out whether I really would or could leave my high-paying job with Disney to make a happier and more purposeful life—and as Kyle was clearly benefiting from his visits with Emma, I finally broke. "Fine," I said. "But you have to make the appointment."

And he did, and I went, and I am so glad that I did.

From the first moment of sitting down with Emma—an extraordinarily beautiful woman of indeterminate age, with platinum hair and the kindest eyes you will ever gaze into—I knew that I had been wrong to be skeptical. Although she would not have been miscast as Cinderella's fairy god-mother—she is like every fantasy you've ever had of a kind-souled auntie who would hold your hand and magically make your problems go away—she was, in person, very grounded and very sensible. And it was immediately clear that her particular magic was, in fact, very practical: she just paid attention and applied her unique powers of insight to what she learned from paying attention. I won't go into the details of what those sessions with Emma were like—they were deeply personal, almost sacred—but I will say this: they worked. More than that, they were life changing. Within a few months I had decided to leave Disney and pursue bigger things, and for the first time in a long time, I felt light. And happy. And powerful.

I came away fully believing in the power of feminine magic. Emma's unique magic draws not from some mysterious supernatural talent but rather from a deep well of feminine intuition and a powerful connection to her own wisdom. Her power isn't spells and potions (the essential oils in her shop notwithstanding)—it's the power of women's ways of knowing, trusted and felt and understood and put into practice. And it's all the more powerful because she shares it.

Call it wisdom, call it magic, call it women's witchy ways—I no longer care what it's called or whether it comes with crystals. It's real, and it's amazing.

(And if you're ever in greater Los Angeles, look Emma up. You won't regret it.)

I don't care how much intellectual knowledge we have. Sometimes intellectual knowledge gets in the way. For example, say you're going to host this meeting, but you can sense people aren't on board with the concept. So what I do in my meetings is, I bridge that. I'll feel the resistance. I'll feel who are my allies in the room, and then I immediately start thinking, How am I going to bring us to a point where we all understand each other? That's fun. It's exciting, and that's what women do.

—Dawn Cartwright, Tantric visionary

For pretty much all of human history, women have been recognized as having unique ways of knowing. They have been identified as oracles, mystics, witches, and seers; their real or perceived powers of insight, foresight, and vision have been fodder for legend, myth, and fairy tale, as well as part of the historical record. This feminine power has sometimes been revered—the Delphic Oracle (the Pythia) was the highest spiritual authority in the otherwise male-dominated world of ancient Greece—but it has more often been derogated and even (sometimes literally) demonized. We all know the stories of "witches" being drowned and burned at the stake, but this grim history reaches beyond Salem and the Puritans back as far as the ancient world. Some of humankind's oldest laws pertain to the punishment of sorcery (all the way to the code of Hammurabi), and the famous dictum "Thou shalt not suffer a witch to live" is from Exodus in the Old Testament.

DID YOU KNOW? One of the oldest stories of witchcraft comes from the Old Testament. 1 Samuel tells the story of the Witch of Endor, whom King Saul asked to summon the spirit of the dead prophet Samuel to help him defeat the Philistines. (It didn't work. Witchy powers have their limits.)

Not all witches, oracles, seers, and mystics in history and folklore have been women, but the differences in treatment and characterization between women and men with the same extraordinary gifts tell the real tale of feminine wisdom and intuition. Consider the status of medicine men and priests over witches and mystics or the different historical and literary treatment of witches and wizards. You've never heard of a "wizard hunt," have you? And what would fairy tales be without crones and hags and—again—wicked witches? The demonization of powerful women—literally, women with unique or special powers—has persisted, with few exceptions, throughout human history and has had a real effect on the place of women in public life.

And it's had a real effect on our contemporary understanding and appreciation of "feminine" ways of knowing. These are most often associated with intuition and other intangible forms of insight—which we tend to distrust, because they don't accord with established (masculine) systems of knowledge.[1] We prefer our knowledge codified and measurable, recorded in books, and proven according to established practices. "Soft" knowledge—that rooted in insight, empathy, and intuition—is often ignored, disregarded, or mocked. That's why Catherine was so skeptical of the idea of a female intuitive as a potential source of healing and support.

But our intuition and emotional insight enable us to understand, explain, see, anticipate, and internalize experiences. Granted, this is often uncomfortable—for us and often for others (who hasn't had the experience of "spooking" somebody with an insight?). But it's uncomfortable precisely because we have, as a culture, denied legitimacy to these special, feminine ways of knowing. It's not because these defy explanation and are too mysterious—it doesn't take much exploration to see how very grounded and real these powers are—it's because we've just become so acculturated to distrusting them.

What would happen if we agreed to give those powers a chance?

Why should we trust these powers? Because they're rooted in very tangible and practical realities. Your "sixth sense" isn't extrasensory—it's supersensory. Your ability to draw insight from what seems intangible or mysterious is in fact just heightened sensory ability: you're using your finely honed skills of observation to pick up on cues that others miss. You're seeing the hint of fear in a friend's eye, hearing an imperceptible quiver in a voice, noting a single bead of nervous sweat, and very quickly drawing from those a number of informed conclusions. You might not even be tracking exactly what cues you're processing—but you're processing them nonetheless.

Intuition is always right in at least two important ways. It is always in response to something. It always has your best interest at heart.

—*GAVIN DE BECKER*, THE GIFT OF FEAR: SURVIVAL SIGNALS THAT PROTECT US FROM VIOLENCE

Research on nonverbal communication skills has clearly shown that women are better than men at reading facial expressions. Because of that, women can pick up on subtler emotional messages. (Research also shows that women can better express emotions, especially positive ones, through facial expressions, tone of voice, and body language. In short, we're just better at sharing and reading subtle social and emotional cues.)[2]

Intuitive and author Jill Willard explains why this is a disproportionately feminine ability (she does insist that some men experience it too):

The right side of the prefrontal cortex is our feminine, or present side, and that's the side where I think some women open quicker than men because we're just more feminine naturally. Or we've learned to be more present than some males, but a lot of females have gotten very left-brained, so you're not even in that right prefrontal cortex, which is the really high intuition because it's the side of the body that integrates it into the present. So you can be like "Oh, I think I know this over there" and then your right side of the prefrontal cortex goes, "Yep," and it's like you have a husband-and-wife team in your intuition. It's important to have the left side too because it brings it to earth and makes it a doing action. You need both sides, but the right side is kind of the "Oh honey, I think something is going on there." You can picture it like a husband-and-wife team in yourself—you need the masculine "doing" side of intuition so you can also do something about the intuition, but you want that right side, the gentle graceful side that just knows it to be true and it's okay.

Willard also explains another reason why this ability is sometimes disparaged. Because we're taking a moment to observe (and tap into our intuition), we're perceived as slow.

Awareness can be perceived as being slow. We're so about winning the race, so if you're aware, and you pause to look around, you get "left behind." When we're more aware, you actually can't do things as quickly, and you're also tucked into your creative side. You could even be at a bar with friends and you're not looking around because you're so present. But then they wonder "Are you uninterested? Are you checking out?" And a lot of kids get it in school, people get it in sports. Like if you're not following in line and doing the militant, patriarchal side of things, then are you weak or are you lacking? Are you not paying attention?

It's amazing how often we have an idea or something crosses our mind, and instead of acknowledging and acting on it, we suppress it and in some cases subconsciously give ourselves a hard time for it ("What a dumb idea!" "Why did I even think about it that way?" "I'm totally overthinking this!").

What if instead of listening to all of these voices, we actually paid closer attention to our intuition? What would happen? We would make better decisions! We would live in a flow state more of the time! We would be healthier mentally and physically!

Willard confirms this: "If we have flow in our body, we have chi energy, we're flowing, our gut health is good, our blood is strong, our heart rate is positive. So even the flow biologically, physically is so good when we're in our feminine because we're flowing. Our menstrual cycle is very healthy, even menopause isn't even that intense because our hormones are regulated. The present side, or the spiritual emotional side, you're more aware of yourself so you know what feels right for you and what doesn't. The gut really knows."

We know things! We are more aware and in tune. We can understand people, motivations, and behaviors before, during, and after they happen.

Sounds like magic to us.

To me, a witch is a woman that is capable of letting her intuition take hold of her actions, that communes with her environment, that isn't afraid of facing challenges.
—PAULO COELHO, BRAZILIAN LYRICIST AND NOVELIST

USE YOUR INTUITIVE POWER

Pause. Jill Willard talks about the power of the pause:

> Pause is so big . . . we call it the witness. I know Michael
> Singer calls it that. I used to call it watching yourself, or
> witnessing yourself. It's noticing that you are not your
> thoughts, you're not your fear, you're not your memory.
> It's starting to watch ourselves and go "Wait a second, I
> just watched myself, and so what's watching that? Is that
> my soul? Is that part of my intuition? Is that my higher
> self? Whatever you want to call it. But start to understand
> that's within you.

Pay attention. When a seemingly random thought crosses
your mind, observe it. Ask where it came from and why. Recognize that it may be there for a reason. And lean in!

Feel it in your body. When you're experiencing an emotional reaction—joy, pain, fear, love—where is it coming from
in your body? Even the process of stopping to feel it gives you
a moment to contemplate what it is and what it means. Is there
pain in your throat? Does this mean you aren't speaking your
truth? Is your stomach in knots? Are you not following your gut
instincts?

What's interesting to me is even when you really look into the feminine and what we've been gifted, regardless of whether we choose to exercise it, but looking at the power and the miracle of life. That our bodies are capable of a miraculous thing and also a wildly fucking painful and traumatic thing. We were gifted both of those. Both the miraculous and the horrific, together.

There was a meme that I posted and had to do with the power of the pussy, and it's so interesting because when did pussy become synonymous for weak? I actually think the attributes of a woman, of what we're capable of doing, are arguably the most powerful, not only from bringing life into the world but to endure. My mom had five kids all naturally. Do you even know what I'm capable of?

I think [femininity] has been so hijacked, and maybe this is the opportunity, and maybe this book is the invitation and the opportunity and permission for us to take back what we already know to be true, which is femininity is quite literally synonymous with powerful.

—ALEXIS JONES, FOUNDER, I AM THAT GIRL

CHAPTER 6

EXPRESS YOURSELF!

What is it about us lady authors and our fascination for the exclamation mark?

—E. A. BUCCHIANERI, AUTHOR

It's become a pretty common piece of career advice for women in the early twenty-first century: Watch your communication style. Don't use cutesy terminology or smiley face emojis in emails, don't be apologetic (see Chapter 12!), don't use the word "just," and don't—whatever you do—use exclamation points in speech or in text. Don't, in other words, be too expressive. Don't let human emotion creep into your everyday business communications.

This is, on some levels, reasonable advice. Cutesiness and excessive enthusiasm can absolutely work against you: when you want to be taken seriously, you need to comport yourself seriously. And over-expressiveness can come across not just as unserious but as inauthentic: Were you really thrilled to get that third-quarter profit and loss statement? Would you blow kisses and give hugs (xoxo!) if you were saying good-bye to a colleague after an in-person meeting? How you communicate is definitely something to be mindful of.

CATHERINE'S STORY

I came of age before the advent of emojis, so in my formative years professionally, I didn't have to grapple with the question of whether smiley faces were appropriate in work or other professional communications. But I do remember the joy of passing crumpled notes to friends in class, with emphatic messages about whatever-the-heck (boys, parents, what to do after school), all underlined and exclamation-pointed and sometimes circled for extra emphasis.

These were private communications, of course—prototexts never meant for the eyes of friends (interception by annoyed math teachers notwithstanding). But I recognized their essential form in the public communication style of my young team at *Babble*. I'd dealt with the enthusiastic communication styles of people younger than me before, of course—many university students have a discomfiting tendency to communicate with their instructors in the same way they do with their peers ("Hey teach! Can u change my grade?!?!")—but not until I was managing a group of (mostly) young women and exchanging volumes of chats, emails, and messages did I begin to understand this as a form.

It was awkward at first, because the smiley faces and shorthand and excessive exclamation points in some ways read to me just like my ninth-grade pass-notes. My first instinct was to try to rein it in—to encourage more formal emails with fewer exclamation points. But I very quickly realized that this didn't serve any helpful purpose. The quick, casual, enthusiastic bursts of communication facilitated open dialog and creative exchange. The bantering quality of written messages fostered warmth and connection. The exclamation points kept enthusiasm up—and when a message came through without them, I came to understand immediately that something wasn't right.

Of course, I counseled my young employees to be mindful of their communication style outside their circle of workmates and to know when and how to deploy or not deploy an exclamation point or "xoxo." But I learned from them that where exclamation points flourish, so too does a kind of joy.

Communication preferences carry a lot of gender baggage. Being expressive is associated with femininity (not just women—consider caricatures of gay men as flamboyant in their communication style), and not in a positive way. Exclamation and expressed enthusiasm are considered girlish. They're screaming teenagers at a Taylor Swift concert and emoji-filled texts. They're clutched pearls and waved hankies and, once upon a time, fainting couches. They're squeals of delight and expressions of love, real or feigned. They're a mode of communication that feels—and often is—filled with emotion. And this isn't just cultural gender bias—effusiveness is a feminine mode of communication. According to psychotherapist Susan Sherwood, women really are more likely than men to use nonverbal modes of communication, such as overt gesturing, eye contact, and animated facial expressions. And linguistics professor Deborah Tannen has pointed out that women, more than men, are conversational punctuators, using small verbal cues like "ah" or "mm-hmm" to indicate emotional acknowledgment. It doesn't just seem like we use more emojis and exclamation points: we actually do use expressive punctuation, even when speaking aloud.

And because this kind of emotional communication has been so long associated with the private sphere—with the conversations between women around kitchen tables and over garden fences—expressions of love and care and communication of feelings in

I think our true nature is to be candid, is to be honest, is to be forthright. I think that those are really beautiful attributes of humanity, which clearly exist inside of women.

—ALEXIS JONES, FOUNDER, I AM THAT GIRL

It's powerful to be expressive because expression is energy. It's thought and feeling asserted and affirmed. It claims space. It generates a force. It makes meaning.

—AMY ROSENTHAL, CREATIVE DIRECTOR, MODEL10ELECTRA

general have also long been considered appropriate only in that sphere, in the domain of house and home. You express love to friends and family. You share your excitement behind closed doors. You exclaim and enthuse in private conversation. In public, however, you treat conversation soberly and seriously.

Thus we tend to think of any form of overexpressiveness as feminine—because it used to occur only in private. Accordingly, it's not deemed suitable for the (more serious, more important) public sphere—the realm of business, politics, and civic dialog.

But does "feminine" expressiveness really have no place in the public sphere? Should women really work to contain and control it if they're to be taken seriously?

Humans are social animals, which means we make meaning through communication (see Chapter 4 on being chatty!). And we communicate through more than just speech; we communicate through laughter and tears, gesture and touch, movement and facial expression. We smile, we frown, we fold our arms over our chests. We punctuate physical movements with sound—we roll our eyes and sigh. We punctuate sound with physical movements—we say, "Wow!" and widen our eyes. We are, in other words, always expressing much, much more than just ideas and directions. No human communication is devoid of emotional expression. The idea that certain expressive flourishes are primarily the habit or practice of one sex is, frankly, sexist.

DID YOU KNOW? Emojis aren't just an artifact of Internet communication: they're part of a much longer history of visual communication. Pictographs–pictures that resemble the object, idea, or feeling they are intended to signify–date back to ancient civilizations, like Sumer, Egypt, and China, and continue to be used in contexts far beyond signaling to your BFF that her last text made you laugh out loud. We've always reached beyond words to express ourselves!

Even if we accept, however, that everyone uses overt expressiveness, does that undermine the suggestion that it is inappropriate for certain kinds of formal communication? Of course not. It's simply a well-accepted norm that we adjust our communication patterns in different social contexts. Cursing is very normal, but we don't do it in church or high-level business meetings (most of us don't, anyway). Similarly we usually keep hugs and high-fives out of very formal conversations: you don't hug a federal court judge or high-five a priest.

But what's wrong, really, with a little more expressiveness within reason? Consider the purpose of punctuation: it underscores meaning. A period simply finishes a thought; an exclamation point asserts it and declares it exciting or interesting. An email that starts with an unadorned "Hello" simply signals the start of a conversation—it tells the reader nothing, other than that the communication is, in fact, hewing to some formality. But "Hello!"—exclamation point asserted—signals that the writer is reaching out with some enthusiasm. Sometimes that's nice—or even valuable—to know.

Of course, there is a time and place for enthusiasm, and obviously false or inauthentic enthusiasm can be off-putting, especially in more formal environments. We need to fully understand the context of our communication and know the audience for it. But as social animals, we crave meaningful communication and are gratified when it is embedded with clear cues and signals. Especially in today's digital world, when there's so much room for miscommunication (in texts and emails), we would all benefit from more awareness, attention, and intention in how we communicate with each other.

And we're happier when we communicate clearly and honestly. It feels good to greet a friend or admired colleague warmly. It boosts our well-being when we express happiness and excitement, even—sometimes especially—when we're not deeply feeling it. Studies have shown that smiling when you're down can lift your mood. Adopting a happy tone in speech or writing

Enthusiasm is contagious. Be a carrier.

—SUSAN RABIN, AUTHOR, DIRECTOR OF THE SCHOOL OF FLIRTING

can do the same. And by expressing ourselves in an enthusiastic or joyful way, we open the door for others to do so as well, leading to a more positive interaction across the board.

If it's "feminine" to enjoy the art of communication and to provide the cues and signals that we all look for, then this is another feminine practice that more people would do well to embrace.

So, go ahead, and (mindfully!) use those exclamation points and other expressions of feeling. Enjoy the full palette of communication tools that you have, and practice using them well. Appropriate and thoughtful expressiveness can make you a better communicator and relationship builder—and a happier person.

USE YOUR ENTHUSIASM

Look for places to add a little love. Be conscious of times—in both work and personal communication—when you might add a little extra enthusiasm to make someone feel good. Free yourself (within reason, of course!) to express yourself more fully and openly, knowing that you'll be bringing a smile to someone's face.

Keep it real. Remember that exclamation points and emojis won't be appropriate in every form of communication. Ask yourself whether you would exclaim if the communication happened in person. If you're tempted to sign off with an "xo," consider whether you'd hug or blow a kiss to the recipient. No? Then use a more traditional sign-off.

Learn from your youngers. Take a closer look at those texts your niece sends you—the ones that seem like they're written in hieroglyphics because of all the emojis. Don't dismiss that style of communication out of hand. Give these texts another read and notice how creative they are. You don't necessarily have to adopt this style, but it's worth watching how communication styles evolve.

Our Favorite Expressive Icons:

Lucille Ball
Diane Keaton
Cher
Marianne Williamson
Aretha Franklin

I encourage women to bring femininity to the boardroom. We talk a lot about the masculine and feminine archetypes, or characteristics, or traits, of leadership, and I think we have different styles of leadership. Masculine characteristics in general are more linear, directive, aggressive, assertive, mathematical. Feminine characteristics of leadership are more emotive, nurturing, collaborative, supportive. We are the power of the "we." The masculine is more "I did this, I did that." And women are always "We, we, we," because we realize that the power of the team is diversity, not of gender, race, or age, but diversity of mind-set and thought leadership. And the best teams have different kinds of skills and thought leadership at the table. And what people don't really understand is, if we were all the same, then companies wouldn't evolve. But the best business success is the tension of thought leadership where we all contribute. But what that requires is discovering what your strength is, owning your strength, celebrating your strength, bringing it to the table, and finding others around you that complement that strength. And so when it comes to femininity in the boardroom, I talk a lot about bringing emotion to the boardroom. Bringing passion to the boardroom. Bringing purpose to the boardroom. Caring about your people, and understanding that the success of companies is not how pretty your building looks, but it's how successfully your team operates together. And it's the togetherness that matters a lot.

—SHELLEY ZALIS, THE FEMALE QUOTIENT

CHAPTER 7

OWN YOUR SEXUAL POWER

> If a woman loves her own body, she doesn't grudge what other
> women do with theirs; if she loves femaleness, she champions
> its rights.
>
> —Naomi Wolff,
> American author, journalist

Female sexual power has been a charged topic from the beginning. What is the story of Adam and Eve about, after all, if not a
woman making the first move? Judeo-Christian history and theology
are full of tales of women whose sexual power caused the downfall of
nations and peoples—as are the mythologies and histories of other
cultures. From the Hindus' Mohini to the Greeks' Sirens to the Old
Testament's Jezebel, Delilah, and Salome—the list is long and fascinating. These were undeniably powerful women, but their power
was (and to some extent still is) considered dangerous and disruptive.

It's not hard to figure out why: women's sexual power has long
been directly associated with men's sexual weakness. Delilah's cutting of Samson's hair is a figurative castration: a sexually powerful
woman can rob a man of his strength and will and render him vulnerable. This idea surfaces in myths and legends about succubae and
Sirens, believed to overcome men and steal their power (and, not
incidentally, their semen) and, in some cases, their lives. Earlier
cultures viewed a man's falling under the influence of a woman as

so disempowering that it could only be the work of demons or other supernatural forces.

Much of this is simple human dynamics. Even if you set aside the hypothesis (asserted by many) that men are naturally power seeking and so inclined to worry about preserving their own power, it's not hard to wrap our heads around the idea that people are uncomfortable with weakness (see our chapter on that topic). Falling under the sexual thrall of another person absolutely can make one feel vulnerable and, like Samson, robbed of strength. Some scholars have suggested that men's aversion to women's sexual independence and power is an evolutionary imperative: sexually powerful women might not limit themselves to one partner, complicating men's ability to ensure that any offspring are truly their own and thus perpetuate their own genetic line. (This is not an unwarranted fear: studies have shown that sexually empowered women are more likely to be "sociosexually unrestricted"—that is, to seek out multiple partners.) Not just science but mythology, literature, and art have explored this idea: the tragedy of the cuckold (who persists to the present day in the idea of the "cuck") is that, sexually duped by a woman, he can't know who his real children are. (That this became the basis for *The Maury Povich Show* is arguably a compounded tragedy.)

AMY'S STORY

I grew up in a sheltered environment. It played out in a number of ways, one being that I was told I should wait until marriage to have sex. (Thankfully I didn't follow that path, or I would still be waiting!) Needless to say, I was shy around boys and, in some ways, a late bloomer.

From early on, I've always loved lingerie. While I was growing up, my mom would give me some of her beautiful French bras and nightgowns. Once I moved to New York City, I made frequent stops at a precious shop on the Upper West Side called Laina Jane (it's still there, and Laina is as lovely as ever). I'd drop in regularly to check out the newest styles and, over the years, built up quite a collection.

Maybe lingerie was—and still is—an escape and a way of playing out fantasies. Lingerie sparks my imagination. It takes me into a fantasy world. When I'm wearing it, I feel powerful and ready for anything that might come my way. Every detail of my outfit, from the lingerie outward, has been considered.

I love that I have something so girly, pretty, and fun . . . just for me. Of course it's nice when my guys appreciate the lingerie, but there's something about having beautiful feminine belongings just for myself—and wearing them when I want to feel a certain way.

For me, my (now not-so-secret) lingerie obsession is a source of inspiration. And feminine power.

Cosmo magazine is packed with bold, provocative, sexy, strong, and sensual images. And yes, we still use a good amount of pink and red. Somehow, when you're talking about sex, love, and power, you can't escape that palette.

—MICHELE PROMAULAYKO, EDITOR IN CHIEF, COSMOPOLITAN

Women's sexual power has long been framed as not just problematic but dangerous—and in need of social control. Feminists have been arguing for years that political efforts to restrict access to birth control and abortion are at their root attempts to control female sexuality. (This is, not incidentally, the entire plot of Margaret Atwood's *The Handmaid's Tale*, a story written in 1985 that, decades later, feels disturbingly prescient.) But whereas reproductive legislation is an overt effort to control female sexuality, the covert efforts—the social and cultural vilification and shaming of female sexuality—have been most effective. The idea that women shouldn't be sexually empowered runs so deep that we often don't realize how much it influences us.

Take the notion of the "slut" and the double standard it purveys. According to author and journalist Peggy Orenstein, "A sexually active girl [or woman] is a slut while a similar boy

[man] is a player." Apart from "player," we don't really have terms for the sexually active boy or man; for girls and women, however, we have "slut," "whore," "slag," "slattern," and (for older women) "cougar," among a host of others. And although we overtly shame unabashedly sexual women (think of how much vitriol gets aimed at Kim Kardashian), we also vilify the so-called prude who suppresses her sexuality. To say that these double standards and contradictions create a confusing landscape for girls and women is to understate things dramatically. (Tantric visionary Dawn Cartwright argues that culturally we skew more prudish than sexual. Women owning their sexual power is considered taboo, she says; hence our suppression of it.)

The very real fears girls and women have about sexual exploitation and abuse complicate this all the more. Women have been told for millennia that they are responsible for men's sexual weakness, that they are the Eves to their Adams, the Delilahs to their Samsons, and that they must rightfully bear the consequences of men's loss of control and efforts to reclaim their sexual power. We have been taught that sexual modesty and prudence will keep us safe, even though research (and experience) tells us that they won't. Study after study has shown that rape and sexual assault are more often demonstrations of power than manifestations of sexual weakness (that is, men don't usually rape because they can't control their sexual urges in response to sexually alluring women; they do it as an exercise of dominance). Given this deeply entrenched history, especially in the era of Harvey Weinstein and #metoo, how can we claim and own our sexual power? How can we use it in a way that promotes our emotional, spiritual, and physical well-being?

There's no question that our sexuality serves us. It is an important part of who we are and deeply connected to our relationship not just to our bodies but to our minds and spirits. Teacher, author, and lecturer Marianne Williamson points out that for women, sexuality is a kind of openness—and so a kind of vulnerability—and in that way it is like spirituality. The "spiritualization process," she says, "is 'I am open.'" In the same way that we need to be spiritually open to be in touch with our spiritual power, we need to be physically open to be in touch with our sexual power.

> Athena is a warrior and achiever, but she's a virgin goddess. Her sister Aphrodite is the love goddess. The good thing about the Greek goddess archetypes is that you don't have to choose; you can embody as many as you're willing to inhabit, whatever aspect of self you're willing to make psychic space for. But for a woman to be happy, I think we need both.
> —MARIANNE WILLIAMSON, SPIRITUAL TEACHER,
> AUTHOR, AND LECTURER

Sexual power doesn't need to manifest in overt sexual openness, however. Sexual expression will differ for each of us. Some expressions of sexual power can emerge in how we dress or move. Others can be private, reserved, kept behind closed doors. We can claim sexual power simply in our connection to our own bodies, in our comfort with and awareness of our physical selves. We can also, crucially, claim it in our connection to the physical world more broadly—to the beauty of others (however defined) and that of the world around us. The eroticism of appreciating things in a manner that connects us to those things is one of the oldest and richest human experiences, and it is not necessarily explicitly sexual. Sipping a glass of fine wine, for example, can be an erotic experience, when it's properly, physically appreciated. So can taking a dip in a warm pool or watching a sunset.

Appreciating the erotic involves more than just leaning into sensuality (although that too can be an important element of finding and staying connected to your sexual power). Eros, of course, in the oldest sense, refers to physical love between actual or potential sexual partners, but it also refers to a force that transcends the physical. For Plato, for example, Eros included a desire to connect with beauty in its truest and purest forms,

I like being a girl. I like dressing girly. I like making myself look pretty. For me, but also for my man. I feel connected to my feminine; I like exuding feminine sexuality—not on the street but with my husband. I like being seductive and feminine in that way.

—JODI GUBER BRUFSKY, FOUNDER, BEYOND YOGA

fueled by appreciation of the manifest forms of beauty (and the "true" form of beauty that underlies all things). Carl Jung's understanding of Eros borrowed from Plato's—he framed it as a desire for wholeness and "psychic relatedness." Sigmund Freud saw it as a kind of life force—a spiritual drive to live. All of these perspectives have in common an understanding of the erotic as a kind of will or aspiration to connect—to beauty, to others, and to life itself.

Viewed this way, owning one's sexual power can serve as a means to connect to one's own body and spirit and bring these in harmony with the rest of the world and other people. Such ownership entails being aware of and purposeful with one's own erotic energy and directing it consciously and deliberately. It means taking responsibility for that power and that energy and using it in connection with others' power and energy in productive and positive ways. And that requires considering both what that power means to you and what it might look like to others. Perhaps others won't even be aware of how you're practicing your sexual power; perhaps your sexual power is the power of private connection to your erotic self.

Practicing awareness and intention around our sexual power—leaning into the integrity of our erotic selves—means taking ownership of and responsibility for that power. And doing this will make us stronger and more connected—to ourselves and to others. And we all want that, right?

OWNING YOUR SEXUAL POWER

Practice the skill of erotic observation. Explore what it feels like to "love" a sunset or the curve of smoke above a fire—and cultivate connection to beauty everywhere you find it. Your erotic self is defined by its connection to beauty and spirit in all forms, so being in touch with your erotic—and, by extension, sexual—power requires practicing appreciation of those things outside the sphere of sex and romance.

Use your senses. Sexuality is a power of the mind but also, of course, of the body, and so the practiced exercise of sexual power requires connection to the senses. But this isn't restricted to the sexual experiences of the senses—on the contrary, honing your senses more broadly can only enhance more, um, *specific* sensual experiences. Pay attention to what delights your senses. Is it the taste of fine wine or great chocolate? Is it the warmth of crackling fires, the feel of wind in your hair, the tingling of your muscles after a run? Do more of that. Find more of that.

Own your physicality. The way you sit, the way you walk— every movement plays into your sexual power. How can this work to your advantage? How can you express yourself intentionally through your movement? Pilates is a great way to get really specific with your various body parts and learn how to move and control them. Dance allows you to free and express yourself. Bring attention to how you're walking down the street and how you feel.

Experiment. Try different ways of expressing and feeling your sensuality and sexuality. See how it feels. Play with it— visit extremes and fantasies. What feels right? Perhaps you'll find you've been playing it too safe, and there's room to indulge. Or maybe you'll find that you want to dial it back. No matter what, the result is clarity and power.

Find inspiration in others. Look to sexual/sensual/erotic role models as a way to find your own approach to sexuality. Consider people across the gender spectrum: Whom do you find sexy? Why? What about that person is sexually or erotically compelling? Is it his or her physical beauty or sense of style, intelligence or charisma? Understanding what we find erotic— what we desire—can help us find our own sexual being.

Love is blind, they say; sex is impervious to reason and mocks the power of all philosophers. But, in fact, a person's sexual choice is the result and sum of their fundamental convictions. Tell me what a person finds sexually attractive and I will tell you their entire philosophy of life.

—AYN RAND, RUSSIAN-AMERICAN NOVELIST, PHILOSOPHER, PLAYWRIGHT, AND SCREENWRITER

I used to think I had to conform to what other people thought femininity was, but my natural, comfortable self is wearing leggings and wearing fitness clothes. Yeah, I like to dress up and look feminine, but now I feel like I can feel feminine doing that as well and being comfortable and not have to wear a full face of makeup and lipstick and all of that in order to feel girly and feminine. Just being surrounded by a team of other athletes and coaches who support that too, that's made a big difference; having other people who think that way and encourage it and support it. Having a community of people who embrace a lot of different styles of gymnastics and diversity: if you look at any of the college gymnastics teams, we're the most unique and diverse because we play to strengths, but all the strengths are feminine in their own way. Being surrounded by that and being a part of that community who believes that for five years now, it's changed the way I view being feminine. Because I can wear a sporty outfit and feel feminine, or I can dress up and still feel the same level of femininity, I think.

—JORDYN WIEBER, OLYMPIC GYMNAST

CHAPTER 8

FLIRT FREELY

I love to flirt, and I've never met a man I didn't like.

—DOLLY PARTON,
SINGER AND SONGWRITER

The history of the word "flirt" is uncertain. The *Oxford English Dictionary* associates it with similar-sounding words, like "flick" and "spurt," and suggests that the "fl" and "irt" connote sudden, superficial movement. But it has also been connected to the French word *fleurette* (little flower) and the (purported) practice of dropping flower petals as a mode of seduction. In any case, it has always been associated with signaling social, and sometimes sexual, interest. And although universally acknowledged as a practice among both women and men, flirting has long been disproportionately identified as a feminine behavior. When we hear the word "flirt" used to describe someone, odds are we will assume that person is a woman.

This is primarily because flirting is a kind of coded communication—it's subtle and covert and works through signaling and suggestion rather than through overt expression of interest—and coded communication is associated more with women than with men. Men, as public creatures, are believed to conform to more explicit and assertive models of communication; "private" women are more likely to communicate with codes and signals. Conventional moral standards across cultures reinforce this dichotomy: flirting as a tool for exploring potential romantic or sexual intimacy must, when wielded by women, be covert, because historically women's participation in such intimacies always had to remain private. Hence the stereotype of the coy maiden, batting her eyelashes above a strategically placed fan to signal her interest in the handsome young man across the room.

CATHERINE'S STORY

There's a picture of my mother taken one Christmas morning during the 1990s. She's modeling a fur coat that she's just received as a gift. She's got the coat on over a nightgown, and she's pulled the collar up to her neck with both hands; her shoulder closest to the camera is slightly raised, and she gazes over it at the camera with a half smile, mid-flirt. I swear, you can practically see her eyelashes fluttering. I wasn't there when this picture was taken—at least, I have no memory of it—but the image frequently comes to mind when I think about my mom, because it so perfectly captures her personality. Flirt.

My mother has always been a dyed-in-the-wool charmer. Charm is her social default setting. Sure, she has her serious side—in professional matters, she's all business—but her posture in social settings has always been one of finely calibrated gregariousness designed to win people over. And win people over she does—few people who meet my mom when she's in full charm mode aren't won over by her. So consistent is this for her that it's always been painfully clear when she dislikes or distrusts someone—she turns the charm off and treats that person matter-of-factly. If you ever meet her, know this: if she doesn't try to make you laugh or win you over within the first few minutes, she probably hates you.

I keep using the word "charm" because that's what it is. My mom's mode of flirtation isn't sexual or even romantic—it's a social posture directed, very simply, at charming people. And it isn't simply about making people like her—if she doesn't like you, or if she's even ambivalent about you, my mom will not care one whit whether you like her. Rather, she genuinely loves social interaction. She loves engaging with people and hearing their stories; she loves cultivating intimacies and connecting with people on a meaningful level.

As someone to whom charm does not come easily, it took me a long time to appreciate what an extraordinary power this is. Flirtation, in any of its forms, has never, ever come naturally to me, and so my mom's facility with charm seemed like magic, in a way. I didn't realize until well into adulthood that it wasn't some mysterious gift but a skill that one could cultivate. Sure, to my mom it came naturally, but I learned that even an introvert like me could adopt some of her practices. Take active listening, for example—leaning into whatever the other person is saying and being attentive to the details—and asking questions; looking for points of commonality and forging connection around those; developing a facility for small talk (I still dislike small talk, but I learned how to do it).

I still don't have the next-level charm skills of my mother, but I have cultivated my own lesser version enough to know that they work.

I think that there's something beautiful about women, and there's something beautiful about giggling and about flirting and about getting dolled up and about all of the things that we deem beneath us when we're the powerhouse, founding, CEO entrepreneurs.

—Alexis Jones, cofounder, I Am That Girl

Flirting has never just been about courtship and expressions of sexual interest. Researchers distinguish between courtship and "quasi-courtship" motivations for flirting and place a variety in the latter category. David Dryden Henningsen has identified five nonsexual motivations, including boosting one's self-esteem, exploring the potential of a (sexual or nonsexual) relationship, increasing intimacy in an existing (sexual or non-sexual) relationship, trying to influence or get something from the other person, and—the simplest motivation—having fun.[1] This is important, because it establishes what flirtation is, at its core: a means of exploring and establishing intimacy across a range of social relationships. Many people flirt, in other words, for the same reasons as Catherine's mom: because they genuinely like people and like cultivating relationships with them and because it naturally feels good to do that.

DID YOU KNOW? The fan was extensively used as a means of communication and, therefore, a way of flirting from the sixteenth century onward in some European societies, especially England and Spain. A whole sign language developed around the use of the fan, and etiquette books and magazines were even published on the topic. Charles Francis Badini wrote *The Original Fanology or Ladies' Conversation Fan*, which was published by William Cock in London in 1797.

The possibility of misinterpretation is probably the biggest and longest-standing challenge with flirting. Because of the close association between flirtation and sexual courtship, and because there is so much scope for social discomfort around misread signals in courtship, the stakes are not just high but unusually complicated. And this isn't just a matter of social embarrassment—that "awkward moment" when you realize that the object of your attention is not really interested in you. As Henningsen points out, "Individuals who mistakenly interpret quasi-courtship flirting as courtship initiation could escalate their own behaviors so as to engage in undesired social-sexual behavior. Such escalation could engender sexual coercion in a relationship or sexual harassment in an organizational setting."

Translation: yes, there really is a risk of misread flirtation cues leading to sexual harassment and coercion.

The thing is, of course, that there really is no good reason why flirtation should lead to "undesired social-sexual behavior." If we can agree—and we should—that no sexualized action should be taken in inappropriate settings (e.g., the workplace) and without the express consent of both parties, then the social parameters of flirtation should remain clear. We may not be there yet as a culture—it does still seem that too many men have trouble distinguishing between friendliness and sexual overtures—but we absolutely should strive to get there, not least because women should not bear the onus of responsibility for controlling the social-sexual behavior of men. We should feel free to be openly and unabashedly charming without fear of being misinterpreted, because flirting in its truest sense—expressing interest in social intimacy—is an unqualified social good: it's one very important way that we explore, establish, and cultivate relationships.

Tantra expert Dawn Cartwright says that flirting is even more than this. "When we're flirting," she says, "we're actually bringing out the best in each other. That's what we want to do anyway. The real purpose for flirting with someone is to spark something in them: something that starts to bring out the best in them. You say something to get them to turn toward you, to get them to light up. It's not meant as harassment. I think there's a big difference there. If we're harassing someone, we're actually trying to bring them down, but true flirtation is different. It's a way that we bring out the best in each other." And again, this doesn't have to be sexual: according to Cartwright, flirting is "an opportunity to enter into conversation" with another person. "It doesn't mean I'll be lovers with him, but I don't have to go, 'Ew, don't talk to me.' No. I can engage with this human being and find a bridge."

Longtime flirting coach Susan Rabin agrees: "Flirting is acting playfully, being charming, living in the present. Flirting is really very Zen. You're concentrating on the moment and the

I'm just a natural flirt, but I don't see it in a sexual way. A lot of the time I'm like an overexcited puppy.
—Kylie Minogue, Australian singer and actress

person you're with." Being in the moment and engaging with others in a way that makes it clear you're present and available is how we create meaningful and intimate relationships. Thus the ability to flirt is a power that unlocks all variety of relational and social possibility: the flirt can forge relationships with relatively little effort, but to great gain. After all, who among your friends and colleagues is most likely to have the fullest Rolodex or contact list? That's right—the charming one.

There's also a more personal advantage to adopting a flirtatious posture in life. Consider the other uses of the verb "flirt": to explore and experiment. To be a flirt is to be both intellectually and emotionally curious—and intellectual and emotional curiosity can profoundly enrich your experience of life. To the flirt, things, places, ideas, and people all have the potential to be interesting and amazing—and so all are worth exploring. She enjoys the experience of discovery and of "flirting"— literally and figuratively—with possibility. The flirt, in her way, is the ultimate adventurer, always looking for new horizons to head for.

What's more powerful than that?

USE YOUR CHARM

Flirting is about exploring relationships—and that starts with exploring people. Pay attention to how you're engaging with people. Start with one conversation at a time. What can you do to be more present and in the moment? What can you learn from the other person in that moment—and how can you learn it? By observation or by asking questions? Treat the person you're engaging with as a landscape to discover: How can you best get to know this person in this one conversation?

Make a daily practice of charm. Charm is about cultivating relationships by making people feel good (hence the association with magic spells!). Ask yourself how you can make someone else feel good on any given day. Could it be through a thoughtful compliment or a generous smile? Maybe it's buying a stranger coffee or bringing home flowers for your partner.

Flirt widely. And not just with people: flirt with ideas and opportunities. Treat the world as a space for exploration, and treat exploration as something fun and light. "Flirting" with an idea or a possibility means exploring it lightly; it doesn't promise commitment, and that's the magic. You could flirt with a new idea every day! Imagine how rich your life would become if you did.

Be purposeful in your flirtations. Sure, flirtation is by definition light and exploratory, but it still shouldn't be undertaken mindlessly. That means treating people as equal partners in any exchange and taking their feelings seriously. If someone doesn't respond to your charm, don't force it.

Make eye contact and "smile" contact. Dr. Pat Allen shares this wisdom: "The major organ for men is their eyes. You look in the eyes of a man that may not attract you, it's just interesting. He's got interesting shoes or clothes or something, or you hear him say something, and you look him in the eyes and you smile, and that's all. Smile." We think this goes for connecting with anyone!

Great Flirts in History:

Mae West
Scarlett O'Hara
Cleopatra
Catherine the Great
Clara Bow

I had this very profound shift with this woman, Jules Blaine Davis. She's the "kitchen healer." She is not a licensed therapist, but her whole thing is helping women. She set up this moms' group, and these women came over and they were like, "We don't cook." When we burned our bras, we burned our aprons too—and women became cut off or cut themselves off or became completely fearful or resentful of the kitchen and said don't put me back in the kitchen. I'm that way. My mom is an amazing cook, but I don't want to go to the store. I buy the ingredients, and I refuse to cook them. Jules said, "You need to make the kitchen a place where you can be rather than another place where there's something you need to do." She believes that there's something inherently primal and important about starting a fire, nourishing other people, creating a place of warmth. But the kitchen right now, although it's the heart of the home, it can be cold. So she said, "I work with these women who have the most perfect designer kitchens . . . but the fancier the kitchen, the less they cook." She's said, "It's like the heart is not beating and no one's being nourished. It comes with an incredible amount of shame, particularly for women who have kids." It's the shame of "I should know how to do this, this shouldn't be scary" and also the shame of "I'm not feeding my children." And as Jules says, that's essential. She says, "We're women. We create life. We are containers. We are vessels." Sorry, but biologically we are. Anatomically we are. Unless we are transgender. That is who we are. And pretending like

continues

continued

that's not who we are is also a betrayal of our femininity and a betrayal of our incredible power. (Not that men can't nourish and do that too and be in their feminine, and not that cooking is only feminine . . . it's not to say that either.) But being able to turn on the fire, the fire needs to go on every day, even if it's to make a pot of tea—that's important. Jules has this thing, she calls it wood board love. It's an amazing idea. You just take a cutting board, particularly if you have hungry children, and you just roughly chop anything in your kitchen, leftovers, cheese, fruit, whatever, and you just put it out. Once it's cut, it goes. When you cut that apple up and put it on a board, it's gone. Then it lets you escape their hunger. You have fed them, but they are feeding themselves. It's a really beautiful but subtle point. She's like, "Then you can go take a shower, answer emails or do whatever you want." Have a tea by yourself. It takes away the burden. That's powerful.

—ELISE LOEHNEN,
CHIEF CONTENT OFFICER, GOOP

CHAPTER 9

BE A DREAMER

The future belongs to those who believe in the beauty of their dreams.

—ELEANOR ROOSEVELT,
AMERICAN POLITICIAN, DIPLOMAT, AND ACTIVIST

The teenage girl gazing out the window, daydreaming her way through math class; the housewife, fantasizing about a soap opera hero emerging from her TV screen to whisk her away; young girls playing Barbie or dress-up or gazing raptly at a princess at Disneyland—these are pretty common stereotypes. We call these flights of fancy or fantasy, and we tend to view them through a feminized lens. We look at the fantasy play of girls and boys very differently, and we look at the fantasies of women and men very differently.

Fantasy as an adult cultural genre is cool; it is, in fact, a multi-billion-dollar industry. ComicCon sells out every year; Marvel's superhero fantasies and *Star Wars* heroes' journeys dominate the cinematic market (yes, Rey, the hero of the latest trilogy, is a girl, but she wasn't even included in the *Star Wars*–branded Monopoly game). Female-centered fantasy, on the other hand, has long been regarded as silly. It's princesses and sparkly vampires (remember how reviled the *Twilight* books and movies were, even though they killed on the best-seller lists and at the box office?) and Hallmark and *Fifty Shades of Grey.* It's escapism of a distinctly feminine variety, and as a culture we've tended to stick up our noses at it—even though it fuels a pretty robust industry. (All those romance novels we mention in Chapter 20 generate a lot of dollars.)

CATHERINE'S STORY

I was not at all a practical little girl. I was a dreamer. A fantasist. A girl who sat at her window and gazed at the sky and imagined wild futures and crazy alternate universes. I wrote fantasy stories (my sixth-grade novel about a demon-fighting girl named Kira and her unicorn companion, Illumina, remains unpublished) and drew endless pictures of fairies and magic forests and alien cities. I tapped on mirrors and investigated closets and wardrobes, just in case Wonderland or Narnia was real. I tried to map a navigable route to Neverland.

I'd say that I had my head in the clouds, but that wouldn't be accurate. My entire self was in the clouds. I lived in the clouds.

And my parents encouraged this. My mom did, I think, because she, herself, has always been a fantasist and dreamer. She delights in the wide-eyed fascination of children with all things fantastic, and she decided very early in her career as a mother that part of her job was to keep the eyes of her own children, and those of any children who accidentally wandered into hearing range, as wide as possible. Accordingly, I grew up in a home in which it seemed entirely possible that there were sea creatures living in the plumbing and gnomes hiding in the closets. There were fairies and elves and imps and other magical creatures in the woods behind our house, and they lived in harmony with the animals there—the squirrels and birds I saw every day and the unicorn my mom swore on her life that she saw one moonlit night. I doubted some of this, sure. But I still loved every bit of it.

Of course, as I got older, I became more circumspect about my love of fantasy. I channeled it into more practical endeavors. I studied political philosophy but incorporated study of myth and folklore into that work; I quoted Aesop and the Brothers Grimm and Hans Christian Andersen in otherwise dry academic essays; I became a mother who, like her own mother, told her children many tall tales. Eventually, I became an executive at the Walt Disney Company, and when my mother proclaimed to me that she never, ever thought I'd end up in business, I said, "Neither did I, Mom, but in this business I'm sitting in conference rooms talking about the finer nuances of fairy tales and running 'blue sky' meetings in which the whole purpose is to literally and figuratively 'Dream Big.'"

I'd somehow turned being a dreamer into a career, and even though the Walt Disney Company is part of my past, my future as an entrepreneur depends (perhaps even more) on my capacity for dreaming big—and believing in those dreams. The ability to dream, it turns out, might be the greatest power of all.

It is interesting that we call something good a "dream," but being called a "dreamer" is somewhat of a putdown.

—Vera Nazarian,
author

It's tempting to say that fantasy in general has never been taken seriously in any form—part of the essence of fantasy and daydreams is, after all, that they are escapes from seriousness. And some might argue that masculine forms of fantasy are likewise treated as unserious: *Fifty Shades of Grey* got the big-screen treatment, after all, while porn still languishes in the darker corners of the Internet. And until it hit HBO, *Game of Thrones* had only a nerd following.

But think about the stereotypes: a daydreaming girl has her head in the clouds, whereas the thoughtful boy is more often regarded as an artist at heart or a budding philosopher. She's distracted by unrealistic fantasies; he's thinking deep thoughts. The young girl playing princess provokes our worry: What if she starts to actually believe that she's a princess who should wait for rescue? What if she confuses fantasy with reality and pins her hopes on dreams' really coming true? The young boy playing superhero, on the other hand, is lauded for his imagination and bravery. We worry that the girl who loves fairy tales will grow up only wanting to marry a prince; the boy who loves make-believe, we think, could grow up to be George Lucas.

DID YOU KNOW? The famous French novel *Madame Bovary* by Gustave Flaubert was in part a warning about the perils of women's indulging too much in their love of fantasy. Emma Bovary's love of novels—at the time, considered fantasy stories in which women lived bolder, more exciting lives—is repeatedly cited in the story as a cause of her downfall. That *Madame Bovary* is itself a novel shouldn't be considered a contradiction: it was the good kind! Trust Flaubert!

We're biased against feminine "dreaminess" because we associate it with unrealistic, possibly misguided hopes—that is, with escapism. Feminine fantasy takes root in the perceived dullness of feminine reality: women's and girls' lives are boring, so they daydream to escape them. Women and girls aren't able to actualize their own hopes and expectations, so they resort to fantasy. Women and girls dream; men and boys *do*.

But we know that there's a very real connection between dreaming and doing. Some of the greatest and most productive innovators and creatives in human history have been dreamers. Walt Disney was a dreamer. George Lucas couldn't have dreamed up *Star Wars* if he wasn't. And even though, historically, mostly men have turned their dreams into realities, there's nothing inherently masculine about doing that: given opportunity, women are more than capable of bringing fantasy to life. (J. K. Rowling created one of the most successful fantasy franchises in history—sure, she had to pretend to be a man to do it, but still, *she did it.*) Entire industries—film, television, literature, theme parks, technological innovation—are built on fantasy, and they thrive because creative and innovative people take their own dreams, visions, and fantasies deeply seriously and commit to bringing them to life.

We also know that exercising the imagination and chasing flights of fancy are good for you. They exercise the brain and increase our ability to think creatively. You can't think outside the box if you can't imagine a world outside the box. And imagining a world outside the box requires the time and space that only dreams afford. Entire sections at the bookstore and on Amazon are dedicated to the topics of creativity and invention, and every book on those real or virtual shelves recommends some form of "daydreaming" or "blue sky thinking" or fantastical brainstorming as a motor for creativity and invention. No great inventions could exist without this type of fantasy and dreaming.

> *In mythology and palmistry, the left hand is called the dreamer because the ring finger on the left hand leads directly to the heart. I find it a very poetic idea. And that's why I only wear nail polish on my left ring finger.*
>
> —GLORIA VANDERBILT, FASHION DESIGNER, ARTIST, AND SOCIALITE

> *Every great dream begins with a dreamer. Always remember, you have within you the strength, the patience, and the passion to reach for the stars to change the world.*
>
> —HARRIET TUBMAN, AMERICAN ABOLITIONIST

The young woman who gazes at the clouds, in other words, could be figuring out the next mode of space flight or plotting the next great science fiction series. The princess-costumed girl may become another Walt Disney or a J. K. Rowling. You might be able to dream up a new career or adventure for yourself if you spend some time just letting your mind wander and imagine all sorts of fantastical things. Or maybe you'll just spice up your relationship or solve a creative problem at work. Daydreaming and indulging in fantasies can spark creativity, facilitate problem solving, and allow you to imagine and set goals.

It can also keep you grounded, balanced, and sane. In a world with so much negativity, escapism can be a wonderfully healthy thing.

HOW TO DREAM BIG

Gaze at the clouds. Or the stars, or the birds, or whatever distant objects pull your mind out of its focus on day-to-day details. Take long walks and let your mind wander. Don't worry that this isn't a productive use of time—it is!

Read fairy tales. And myths and folklore and fantasy stories, or watch movies of the same. Let yourself take them seriously, even just for a moment. Let yourself inhabit them. Enter those worlds and really experience how exceptional they are. Think about the extraordinary craft that's required to build a world! The authors and creators of these stories had to take them seriously in order to build them. Ask yourself how you might do the same. Embrace the concept of "what if?" and apply it to your own life, work, or art.

Bring "blue sky" into your professional and creative practice. "Blue sky" thinking is just what it sounds like: a type of thinking/idea generation that blows off the roof and reaches all the way up to the sky. The whole idea is to approach brainstorming from the standpoint that no idea is too wild or crazy or unrealistic—and that, somewhere in the clouds, there's something both totally fantastic and actually doable. So, keep a "blue sky" journal in which you record your wildest and wooliest ideas. Hold meetings in which no idea is off the table. Kick off those meetings (or that journal) with your own craziest idea ("What if we created a dragon, and it flew around our launch party?"—an actual blue sky idea realized at the opening of Disney World's new Fantasyland).

Support other dreamers. Whether it's your employees or your kids or your significant other, encourage others to dream. Realize that while at times it may feel like a little much (or a waste of time or a distraction from what you'd like them to be doing), it may lead to greatness!

Our Favorite Dreamers:

Kathryn Bigelow
Susan B. Anthony
Amelia Earhart
Oprah
Malala Yousafazi
Sally Ride

For me, femininity is about embracing my softness and my vulnerability and seeing those not as a weakness but as my biggest strengths. I spent a lot of time growing up hiding my emotions and my feelings, and my family would never see me cry openly. I would always do it behind closed doors because somewhere along the way, I was ingrained with the idea that feelings are weak. It wasn't until I started really tapping into my feelings that I had actually uncovered my own strength, and I think that's so tied to what femininity is. A lot of it was when I ended up getting into an abusive relationship, and I kept so much hidden. I didn't share any of the pain that I was going through with anyone and was just suffering silently. I remember once I got out of the relationship, my sister actually told me, she said, "I feel like I don't even know you because you don't show any emotion at all. I've never seen you cry, I've never seen you hurt or upset." To have my sister tell me she didn't feel like she knew me was really impactful in a really sad way, and it made me look at all the areas where I had kept things bottled up. Once I started to allow myself to express, there was a period for a year where I became a leaking faucet, where I couldn't turn off the tears, but it was so cathartic, and so emotionally freeing, and so connecting. Once I started sharing the softer, vulnerable side of me—the side of me that had tears and deep compassion and deep empathy, but also deep grief—that's when I really started to make connections with people, and it resonated with people, and it was just this sense of really being authentic. And I'm not alone in what I'm feeling. There are so many other people and women out there that feel exactly the same way.

—LIZ ARCH, YOGI

CHAPTER 10

SURRENDER

One of the most important changes we can make is to shift
from seeing surrender as a sign of defeat, to seeing it as a land
of victory inside ourselves.

—JUDITH ORLOFF,
THE POWER OF SURRENDER

Why do we view surrender as a demonstration of weakness?
Consider the concept of surrender in war: a country or army
that surrenders to another is thought to have lost. One country wins;
the other loses. One side has been proven strong, the other, weak.
Surrender in war and politics means, quite simply, giving up or giving in—which, given the stakes, is deemed indisputably bad.

Surrender in personal or social contexts gets framed in pretty
much the same way: we understand it to mean relinquishing power
and control to someone else. This, of course, may be hard for those
of us with a controlling nature. But as we see in Chapter 18 on being
supportive, not all of us want to be the person who takes charge,
who controls everything. So, maybe it's not always a bad thing to
cede that role. And in any case, we don't think that surrender is
simply about giving up and giving in; nor do we think that doing so
is always a bad thing. Some scholars have tried to reframe surrender
in more positive terms, drawing attention to what they say is the
most important—and most overlooked—component of surrender:

it is literally how fighting ends.[1] And since putting an end to fighting is an indisputable good, shouldn't we rethink surrender as a good as well?

AMY'S STORY

One day, while getting a manicure at my favorite Queen Bee in Culver City, California, one of the facialists who worked there approached me (let's call her Dana). I had been told that in addition to giving great facials, she was also a medium (meaning, she could communicate with spirits and energies beyond this plane—yes, I know this story may sound very "LA"). She asked me if I was interested in messages she was receiving for me, and naturally I said yes. Always.

Dana proceeded to tell me that my heart was closed off and guarded. I was somewhat aware of this, particularly in romantic relationships, and I was working on it. She said I should wear rose quartz around my neck every day to open up my heart. I immediately imagined the cheap rose quartz crystals from Venice Beach boardwalk and thought to myself, No . . . I can't see that happening.

She continued, "You think that everything that happens is because of you. When something good happens, you think it's because you did it. And when something bad happens, you feel worse about it because you think you're the reason." This stung for a moment (the first part). I took it all in. Dana went on, "You've been given gifts to do what you do. When you produce something great for work, that's because of that gift, not because *you* did it, and when you're dealing with a tough situation, that's because you have a lesson to learn."

Not what I was expecting that day but a very powerful message. It meant I could let go. I could continue to work hard and do my best. But I didn't have to attach personal success or failure to everything that happened. This way of thinking takes a lot of pressure off and has affected me ever since. Surrender.

And by the way, one of my dearest friends, an incredible jeweler, created the most beautiful—and I would say magical—one-of-a-kind rose quartz necklace for me. And I have worn it every day since.

Being defensive and combative doesn't really make you stronger.

—GABBY REECE,
ATHLETE, AUTHOR,
AND FITNESS
PERSONALITY

Reframing surrender is not as easy as it sounds. After all, many of us love to feel in control—and many of us are very good at being in control, as we'll discuss in Chapter 17—and so we tend to resist situations where we must relinquish it. But we simply have little or no control over a long list of things in our lives, ranging from how our children respond when we ask them to do their homework to how a friend or lover reacts when we break bad news. Or how quickly we will land the next big business deal for our company. Or when the rain will finally stop . . . or start. You get the idea.

And this is where a masculine posture of dominance can, ironically, become self-defeating. We simply can't control everything—nor should we. And a determination to "win" at all costs can, believe it or not, work against us. "Going down fighting" means exactly that: going down. How much human tragedy results directly from someone's determination to win at all costs? How often has humanity "gone down"?

But what if we took a different approach to the uncontrollable? What if we asserted that ceding control—letting go, releasing hold, saying "enough"—could be powerful? How would the outcomes of struggles of all varieties—not just political or social ones but personal ones—change?

Something amazing happens when we surrender and just love. We melt into another world, a realm of power already within us. The world changes when we change. The world softens when we soften. The world loves us when we choose to love the world.

—MARIANNE WILLIAMSON, SPIRITUAL TEACHER, AUTHOR, AND LECTURER

We all have different views about destiny, karma, or a higher power. No matter what you believe, you may have found yourself in a challenging, upsetting, or even overwhelming situation and reached a point at which you had no choice but to let go. You may have realized that you could do nothing more: things would unfold in a certain way no matter how tightly you held on, and so you made an active, purposeful choice to let go. To give in. To give up.

And we're willing to bet that in some of those circumstances, you felt really good about that choice. Empowered, even. That's because surrender can be powerful. Surrender, after all, requires confidence. It requires that we have some certainty, faith, trust, belief, or knowledge that relinquishing control in that moment is the best course of action and conducive to our longer-term well-being. Surrender can also feel powerful because it is an exercise of our judgment and our ability to assess a situation soberly: we consider what's at stake and make the most reasoned decision.

This becomes all the more meaningful if we agree that sometimes winning or dominating isn't the best result. Once we've decided that there are values and goods beyond winning or not giving up, a whole world of possibility opens up. We assert that dominating and winning are not the most important principles—and that's no small thing.

DID YOU KNOW? The word "surrender" comes from the Middle English *surrendre*, from the French *sur-, sus-,* or *suz* "under" + *rendre* "to give back." Giving back—that has a more positive flavor than you'd expect, right?

And think about what it means to have trust in the bigger picture—it means opening ourselves to a much wider landscape of possibility. We prize our ability to control outcomes, but so many of the best things that happen in life are unexpected, serendipitous, magical. And if we're able to surrender to possibility consistently—not just in those "pushed to the limit" moments—we make those things possible. (We also, not incidentally, allow ourselves to be taken care of and can better conserve our energy for more important things. How much energy have you wasted trying to control things that ultimately didn't matter? If you're like us, probably too much.)

Michael A. Singer explores this idea powerfully in *The Surrender Experiment.* He shares how a life-changing meditation experience caused him to give up the life that he knew—to divorce, move to the middle of nowhere, and start afresh. Through his experiences (one might call them serendipitous moments or even miracles), he practices surrender and learns the power of giving in. He shows how the practice of surrender can introduce ease and gentleness into our experience—and, as a result, a greater sense of peace.

It's a very powerful message. And although Singer is a man, we think it's still a profoundly feminine one. Surrender, as we've already said, recognizes the real value of not pursuing victory and domination. Ceding control brings comfort. And it requires confidence—rooted in feminine intuition and insight, we'd argue—that we can find other paths to success or fulfillment. Any challenge, moment of crisis, or crucial decision point when the question "Can I control this" hangs in the air is a moment when giving up control really could be the best option. These are not only good learning experiences but also necessary to our growth.

And to our power.

HOW TO SOURCE POWER THROUGH SURRENDER

Experiment with surrender. Choose small things to "let go" of. When you're on the verge of honking your horn at someone or sending a frustrated email, skip it. Over time, choose bigger things. And then all things!

Watch closely. What happens when you make a conscious decision to let go? How does it feel? Does the outcome change? More times than not, the outcome will be the same regardless of how you engage with a problem or challenge. If anything, if you adopt an easier, more graceful approach, the outcome will be a more positive one.

Let nature show the way. Take moments to go outside and look at the stars in the sky, majestic mountains, powerful waves, ants building an anthill—anything in nature that reminds you that you are just one piece of a much larger whole. Remember how little we are in the universe and how powerful the universe is because it just does its thing.

My feminine qualities—vulnerability, boldness, unique-ness, authenticity—have had their moments of sending me on a temporary detour, and I've had to find my way back to my original path. It was painful when people re-sponded to my femininity by criticizing me, by putting up barriers, or by creating circumstances to block me. At the same time, it has been those very same qualities that kept me from quitting and giving up on myself. If anything, they've ultimately opened doors that I didn't know existed, and I'm eternally grateful for that.

—PAULA ABDUL,
CHOREOGRAPHER AND POP STAR

CHAPTER 11

BE AGREEABLE

I'm a good girl because I really believe in love, integrity, and respect.

—Katy Perry,
SINGER AND SONGWRITER

Being agreeable should be an unequivocally good thing, right? Agreeability is nice! It's one of those qualities that feels universally good. It's right there in the root word: "agree." Agreement is great! It entails finding common ground, getting in harmony, aligning ideas or opinions. It's certainly better than disagreement or disagreeability, which most of us try to avoid.

Or, at least we say we do. In social and cultural practice, however, we tend to prize a certain degree of combativeness and provocation. This is especially true in the Internet era, where the most provocative opinions get the most attention. Being agreeable—being gently positive in manner, hewing to social politeness, being nice—is acknowledged as pleasant, and, let's face it, feminine. What are little girls made of, after all, if not sugar and spice and everything nice? But while being the "good girl" or "agreeable" is considered (for girls and women) a good thing, it has never been considered powerful. If anything, being too nice has been perceived as the ultimate weakness.

CATHERINE'S STORY

Most people who know me would tell you that I'm a very agreeable person—what my grandmother would have called a classic "good girl." I am unfailingly polite and good-natured. I never, ever lose my temper, possibly because there is no temper to lose. I have excellent manners and am unflaggingly easygoing. I have a keen sense of propriety and almost always know the right thing to say. (Almost. When I do take a misstep, it's spectacular.) I would hold up very well if I ever had occasion to meet the queen. I once heard someone say that I "present well," and although the young burgeoning feminist that I was at the time took umbrage ("I'm *not* a show pony," I raged to a girlfriend—after the fact, of course, because I was far too polite to challenge the speaker in the moment), I came to recognize the power I had: the power of social literacy and of social caring.

Being "good" in the context of the classic good girl really comes down to not just being able to (literally and figuratively) read the room and comport yourself appropriately but actually caring about the import of doing that. Caring about how people interact and wanting them to behave nicely with each other. Getting along with others, being polite, "presenting well" are all social skills born of the ability to take in all the social information at hand and interpret it correctly.

I never actively cultivated this skill. For one thing, I'm Canadian, so a certain amount of agreeability and politeness comes with the heritage. For another, I'm an introvert, so hanging back and reading the room has always come more naturally to me than diving in and socializing. But mostly, I think, as a girl, I learned early and often that social approval was associated with certain codes of feminine behavior—being cooperative, composed, and polite.

Being agreeable. And as an ambitious girl who craved approval, I refined that behavior to maximum effect. If there were gold stars for good behavior—and let's face it, there often are—I was going to get them.

For a time in my college years, I tried to rebel against this training (my aversion to being told that I "present well" was a function of this) because I thought that it was unfeminist to be a "good girl." But I never actually succeeded—that training runs deep—and now I'm very glad that I didn't. Because I now understand this: my social literacy, my agreeability, my "good girl" power is a very real and effective power. It's one that I'm glad to have.

> *My daughter is so powerful, and she's so feminine, and she will kick someone's ass, no problem. But she's also so loving and kind.*
>
> —GABBY REECE, ATHLETE, AUTHOR, AND FITNESS PERSONALITY

As Catherine noted in her story, we do associate agreeability—niceness, politeness, and cooperativeness—with girls and women. We actively encourage girls to be those things. Study after study has shown that girls are told more frequently than boys to play nice and get along. It's even been suggested that ADHD is underdiagnosed in girls because they're so conditioned to be well-behaved and agreeable that the disorder just doesn't manifest in disruptive behavior for them: they behave well even when their brain chemistry is urging them to act out. We expect boys to get into tussles in the schoolyard. We expect girls to get along and behave well in almost all circumstances. And many of them work very hard to conform to that expectation. Hence the stereotype of the "good girl," which is deeply rooted in the very real, long-standing behaviors of girls and women.

DID YOU KNOW? Politeness as a feminine virtue is as old as recorded history, appearing everywhere from the Bible (Proverbs), to Confucianism (*Book of Etiquette and Ceremonial*), to the mores of the ancient Romans.

Because "being good" is so closely associated with femininity, it sometimes gets a bad rap. The sweet-tempered and agreeable "good girl" is often characterized as weak and compliant, compared to the tomboy who isn't afraid to punch a boy in the nose if he bothers her. Good girls don't become leaders in this framing—only tough girls can really break into that role. We also tend to characterize agreeability as inauthentic—the "good girl" is fake; the tough girl is real. We praise Rihanna—"Bad Girl Riri" as she styles herself on social media—as authentic and real but disdain Taylor Swift as saccharine: sweet but fake. Author Rachel Simmons went so far as to call the posture of the good girl a "curse" in *The Curse of the Good Girl.* She said that it "erects a psychological glass ceiling that begins its destructive sprawl in girlhood and extends across the female life span, stunting the growth of skills and habits essential to becoming a strong woman." Yikes.

But is being a good girl really so bad? Of course not.

Simmons isn't wrong when she says that the dominance of the "good girl" stereotype can have—and has had—a problematic impact on the moral and social development of girls and women. The literature on the psychology of girls has pretty well established that the pressure to conform to social norms of polite behavior can have a detrimental effect in a variety of ways: for example, the expectation that girls should always be polite makes it less likely that they will voice disagreement in the classroom; the expectation that they'll be cooperative and friendly may pressure them to sublimate disagreements with other girls, resulting in these being driven underground or channeled into passive-aggressive social behavior (see Lyn Mikel Brown's *Girlfighting* for a great explanation of this). And, of course, the pressure to be agreeable and "nice" has often been cited as a factor in women's discomfort with being assertive in resisting unwanted sexual advances—saying no, after all, might be interpreted as rude.

All that said, however, niceness, politeness, and kindness are obviously not the problem—these are undeniably social positives. The real problem is the framing of the "good girl" as a codified behavioral expectation for girls and women rather than as a powerful posture that they can choose and leverage in the manner that suits them best. When we look at "goodness" as a standard that should apply to humans across the board, we can begin to see how the components of agreeability—which is to say, social goodness—begin to look like underused powers that we would all—girls, boys, men, and women alike—be well-advised to lean into more frequently.

If we look at the "good girl" and her component elements as a model of power that we can tap into when it serves us, she takes on a different cast. The "good girl" isn't nice for niceness's sake; she's not polite simply because she's expected to be. She owns her powers of good, and she uses them because it is good to use them—she is polite because it serves her and her relationships. She recognizes that politeness is an important social tool. She is kind because she recognizes that kindness can yield greater influence than its opposite—and because it feels better to be kind than to be unkind. She is agreeable because she knows that agreeability can be a powerful asset in cultivating and maintaining relationships at work, at home, and in friendship. She knows that agreeable people are pleasant to be around, and she works that to her advantage. And she enjoys it. We all know that it's simply much more pleasant to be agreeable and to be around agreeable people. Shouldn't we all want to cultivate that quality?

So, go ahead, be the good girl. Be agreeable. If you own it and use it purposefully, that agreeability can be a superpower.

Women are able to check our ego. It's still there, the strength is still there, the "I'll cut you" is still there, but we do it so nicely, and so sweetly. That in itself is so powerful, and I think that taking that power back and redefining it for ourselves will continue to change how society perceives all of these things. And then we can restructure the world order.

—CHRISTINE SIMMONS, PRESIDENT AND COO, LA SPARKS

LEAN INTO YOUR AGREEABILITY

Politeness is a skill—and a habit. It improves with use: the more you integrate small acts of politeness into your day-to-day life, the more second nature they'll become (if they're not already!). That means being generous with pleases and thank-yous, of course, as well as other polite acts, like sending thank-you notes and RSVPs (even when they haven't been asked for!), offering a helping hand to that person with too many bags, and being on time.

Be polite even when you're angry. This is when minding your manners is hardest—but also most effective. This doesn't mean don't get angry—it means channel your expression of anger through the filter of good behavior. Take a moment. Breathe. Punch the pillow in private. In public, keep a civil tone; be respectful. And if whomever you're angry at does deserve a stronger reaction, make that call in good conscience and call them out. Good girls aren't passive—they're deliberate.

Practice random acts of kindness. What feels better than a surprising and thoughtful act from a friend or loved one? Each and every day, do at least one thing to show you're thinking of someone else. This could be as simple as sending a "thinking of you" text or flowers. Or dropping off food to the local homeless shelter. Let this goodness flow out of you and positively impact the world. Own it!

Model the values of agreeability. Cooperation, inclusiveness, and accommodation are core components of agreeability as a practice. And these, obviously, can combine to make for a powerful leadership style, among other things. Some of the greatest business leaders have been expert team builders, and their skill at team building has been directly connected to their commitment to those kinds of ideals. It's also a good tactic in parenting!

We get so many contradictory messages in terms of how we should operate as women. "Yes, we should be feminine" but also "No, you can't." "Be yourself but not like this." "Do this but don't do that too much." We get so many different messages. Like there's just no way for us to make everybody happy, we already know that. So I try to separate the two. I try to go in for me and my piece, wear my mask while I'm at work, do what I have to do. I don't necessarily need to lean into my femininity there, for me now, at this stage in my life, maybe later. And then when I go home, the big thing for me about being feminine is trying to incorporate that into a relationship that's nurturing and meaningful.

—Cari Champion,
SportsCenter anchor, ESPN

CHAPTER 12

APOLOGIZE

In some families, please is described as the magic word. In our house, however, it was sorry.

—MARGARET LAURENCE,
CANADIAN NOVELIST

We're admonished from a very young age to say that we're sorry for even minor transgressions. "Say sorry for taking that cookie," we're told, or "Apologize to your sister for pulling her hair." The ability to apologize, we're told—rightly—is part and parcel of being a decent human being.

But as an adult, especially if you're a woman, you may hear something different. Advice columns and career guides tell us to stop apologizing. Don't say sorry; don't ask for pardon or forgiveness; don't even use the word "just" as a qualifier for requests ("I just wanted to ask . . . ") because it may come off as submissive. Don't apologize, that is, if you're a woman. (Canadians, presumably, are off the hook.) In men, apologizing and begging pardon are often seen as charming. In women, they're a sign of weakness.

Why is that? According to advice columns, if you're apologizing, you're putting yourself in a submissive position. If a real apology is in order, that's fine—you're doing what's necessary. But if you're apologizing figuratively, they say, you're signaling deference—and that could damage others' perceptions of you.

AMY'S STORY

I often think about the various relationships that have come and gone in my life. Love relationships that reached their expiration dates. Friendships that dwindled away with time. Work relationships that were mutually beneficial for a period—and then weren't.

For me, it's hard not to have pangs of regret about relationships that have gone south. Regardless of the circumstances, and even if parting ways truly was the best for both parties, I often feel nostalgic and even guilty.

As much as my instinct is always to try to fix or resolve problems, to smooth things over, this isn't always possible. And it's not my responsibility to take it all on as often as I feel the need to do.

In recent years, I've decided to dig deeper into these emotions and, when possible, to proactively clear any negative energy or negative feelings. When a certain past relationship recurs in my thoughts, I explore ways to create closure or a more positive feeling. I might simply reach out and let that person know I'm thinking about him or her. I might write that person a letter (which I can send or not, depending on the circumstances). A positive and unexpected run-in (sometimes I think my thoughts manifest these) might give me the opportunity to unload the energetic baggage I'm carrying. I might apologize for my actions or for any past misunderstandings. Any of these actions could initiate the conversation necessary to create a bridge and remove any negative feelings.

I have realized that I always have the opportunity to create a proactive and positive gesture, big or small. And taking that opportunity is a way to rebuild a relationship or to create necessary, positive closure. The lightness and relief experienced from cleaning and clearing up the past are a tremendous gift. The apology, big or small, can be the powerful way to move things forward.

There's a very important distinction between the two types of apology. The necessary apology, issued in response to a real or perceived harm, is a direct form of communication and a norm that maintains social and relational harmony. And it's powerful. Consider the terrible PR generated when a celebrity or politician delivers a bad apology (there's even a word for these: "nonapologies"). Social harmony requires that when we wrong each other, we acknowledge that and make amends at least symbolically. An honest apology delivered in response to an actual wrong does not put the apologist in a weaker position—it restores balance.

The second type of apology—let's call it a symbolic apology—does put the apologist in a deferential position. That's the whole point, after all. When you say, "I'm sorry to disturb you," or "Sorry this response is so late," or even just "Sorry, excuse me!" when brushing past someone in Starbucks, you're signaling that the other person's time or space is important. In that moment, you're literally deferring to him or her. This is precisely why "being apologetic" so often gets characterized as feminine—it's a deferential posture, and deference is coded more strongly as feminine than as masculine. But deferential or submissive behaviors aren't necessarily weak.

A real apology is a gesture of respect. Why not look at a symbolic apology in the same way? The email that includes "my apologies for taking so long to get back to you" and the spontaneous "sorry" murmured when you bump someone in the coffee line both communicate respect. You respect someone else's time and attention, so you apologize when you might have run afoul (even very marginally!) of those. You respect others' space, so you apologize when you enter it accidentally. Even the passing "Sorry, do you have a minute" uttered when you're sticking your head into a colleague's office or stopping someone in the hallway acknowledges that you value that individual's time.

And respecting other people is anything but weak. It's the glue that holds communities together; it enables trust and

What if my friend that is so important to me decides I'm not worth her time anymore? How many "demerits" will it cost me if I apologize and admit I was wrong? The truth is though, when I have been able to apologize, the friendship has always grown stronger, and I have grown stronger. Apologies are the proof that we are more than the sum of our mistakes.

—Kristen Castree, Marketing Executive

It's powerful to make a good apology because an apology—a real one—states plainly, no matter what specific words are used, "I see, and I care."

—Amy Rosenthal, Creative Director, Model10Electra

support and makes all the wonderful social parts of civil society possible. It's the basis of civility.

There's real power in the proactivity and responsibility associated with an apology. Regardless of the scenario or type of apology, the act of apologizing means you're taking the lead in creating a bond or bridging a gap. You're moving things forward in a positive way. We carry substantial emotional baggage around worrying about others and how they feel. How nice it feels to unload that baggage by addressing it head-on and showing others that you care. An apology creates connection.

So, don't say sorry for saying sorry. Say sorry as much and as often as you like. If your instinct is to be more civil to and respectful of other people, run with it. We could use more of that.

APOLOGIZE WITH POWER

Make your real apologies count. There is such a thing as a good apology: it's one that takes responsibility. The classic "I'm sorry if you felt that way" just doesn't work if some real harm has been done, because it declines responsibility for the action and instead puts the onus on the other person's feelings.

Be generous with your symbolic apologies. These have meaning precisely because they signal respect and communicate awareness of others' boundaries and integrity, and that's a good thing. So, *do* say sorry if you bump someone in the Starbucks line or are interrupting a conversation. It will be appreciated.

Mean it when you say it. There is such a thing as overapologizing. If you begin every sentence with "sorry," your real sorries won't carry as much weight. And if you're really not sorry for a given action, that's fine too—skip it. An insincere apology isn't a good apology either. Your real apologies will carry more weight if you only issue them when you mean them.

My goal isn't to be the most feminine person I can be; my goal is to be my most authentic self. It's about what speaks to me. If this frilly top makes me feel good, then I want to wear it—but I might feel just as feminine in a T-shirt and jeans. To me femininity is an expression of how you feel.

I always say that when little girls play dress up, it isn't because someone is telling them they should dress a certain way; it's just fun to put on their mom's high heels or put on a pink tutu or try makeup. It's fun. I think that it does become pressure for a lot of women, but I just remind women that it's one of the fun things about being a woman. My husband has to pick between one of twenty blue shirts, but I can say, "I feel like wearing a frilly dress today or I feel like wearing a tight skirt or I'm going to wear jeans and a sweater." And same with hair and makeup. Most days I hardly wear any makeup, and don't do a lot with my hair, but I can. But my husband, he can go, what, a half an inch shorter? It's a fun thing that we can express who we are in that day (which, by the way, sometimes I'm five different people in one day!). Over a week I have different moods and different things that I want to say to the world: sometimes I like wearing heels and a skirt, and it's like, I'm badass today; don't mess with me. And other days I'm in my softy beach mode, and that's fun. Some days I don't even want to feel super feminine. Some days I want to be more androgynous because that's how I'm feeling.

What does feminine even mean? I think feminine is a sexy black dress, but I also think feminine is barefoot with jeans on the beach.

—CINDY CRAWFORD, MODEL

CHAPTER 13

EMBRACE GLAMOUR

I don't mind being burdened with being glamorous and sexual. Beauty and femininity are ageless and can't be contrived, and glamour, although the manufacturers won't like this, cannot be manufactured. Not real glamour; it's based on femininity.

—MARILYN MONROE, AMERICAN ACTRESS

Love of glamour is arguably one of the most common and pervasive stereotypes associated with femininity. It's lipstick and glitter, high heels and pretty dresses. It's every image depicting a little girl playing dress-up in her mother's clothing; it's every ad for eyeshadow or perfume. It's Barbie in her heyday, Victoria's Secret Angels in diamond-encrusted lingerie, and Beyoncé on the red carpet (or anywhere, really). It's the love of everything and anything that dazzles and sparkles and beguiles.

CATHERINE'S STORY

When I first started teaching, I hated the uniform. You know what I mean: the professorial look. Rumpled tweeds or sweaters with cheap ties for men; trousers, blazers, and sensible shoes for women. I rejected it entirely.

My teaching uniform was, instead, high-heeled boots. Very high-heeled boots. They were the one nonnegotiable part of my outfit because the boots made me feel powerful. They made me walk straight and stand tall, and when I was standing at a lectern or pacing the front of a seminar room, that mattered. Feeling taller made me feel more confident; each authoritative clomp of my heel assertively punctuated my words.

I didn't realize that this registered in any significant way with my students until a female student mentioned my boots in passing during an office visit. "We love that you wear high heels, you know," she said. We? "A few of us. Girls. It was kind of surprising at first, but we decided it makes the class feel more glamorous. Less boring."

I'm pretty sure that I raised an eyebrow.

"Not boring—your lectures aren't boring. But, you know. Plato could seem boring. But you're dressed up, so it seems more exciting. Than it already is."

I had never in my life imagined that anyone might find me glamorous. And to be fair, my student didn't exactly call me that. But she put her finger on something interesting that I've never forgotten: sometimes adding a little glamour (a little heel, a little something else) makes a whole space feel more important.

Imagine being able to make your whole self feel more important.

Glamorousness is one of the most stereotypical feminine traits around. But historically it hasn't always been associated with women, or even people. In fact, one of the most famous examinations of glamour was a study of the peacock.

The peacock is arguably one of the most glamorous creatures in the animal kingdom. Charles Darwin famously said that the sight of the peacock's tail made him sick, because it represented a conflict (which he eventually overcame) in his theory of evolution: natural versus sexual selection. The peacock's extraordinarily beautiful plumage served no purpose relevant to natural selection, but it did introduce the idea of sexual selection: that creatures, drawn to beauty, would perpetuate a reproduction cycle favoring that quality (as well as health, well-being, etc.). Darwin's problem was that, at least in the case of the peacock, this put sexual choice in the hands of women: because he believed women were inferior, this seemed counterintuitive. ("Till I compare all my notes, I feel very doubtful about the share males and females play in sexual selection; I suspect that the male will pair with any female, and that the females select the most victorious or most beautiful cock, or him with beauty and courage combined," he wrote in late 1859, following the publication of *On the Origin of Species*.)

But the science was undeniable, and Darwin came around: "A girl sees a handsome man and without observing whether his nose or his whiskers are the tenth of an inch longer or shorter than in some other man, admires his appearance and says she will marry him," he wrote in 1868. "So I suppose with the peahen; and the tail has been increased in length merely by on the whole presenting a more gorgeous appearance." Plumage, he discovered, serves a crucial natural purpose: attraction. And the artificial enhancement of plumage—glamour—is the inevitable next evolutionary step. It is, literally, our way of gaming the natural selection cycle.

And human beings have been doing this for pretty much the entirety of their history. The use of adornment to create the illusion of not just beauty but vitality and power is as old as crowns and jewels and gilded shields, and it has been a mainstay of powerful people throughout history (from the ancient Persians through the pre-Revolutionary French and beyond). It's also served much the same purpose as in peacocks: to signal potency and vitality. The dull, unadorned creature is understood to lack something—health or wealth or well-being. Shiny

Whether it be a piece of vintage, fine, or costume jewelry, jewelry brings a sense of empowerment and comfort to women. It has the power to hold a memory of a loved one, a special day, or simply a glimpse of one's style. It is a true and pure vision of who we are and our feminine nature. It is an outer reflection of our inner self.

—TIFFANY BARTOLACCI, COFOUNDER AND DESIGNER, BORGIONI

I don't mind the sparkle—I think it's kind of a tradition in skating. I don't think the men really need sparkles, but for the women, it's part of the glamour of our sport.

—KRISTI YAMAGUCHI, FIGURE SKATER

things—whether brilliant feathers or jewels and finery—signal surplus. They say, "I am a rich and happy creature of abundance."

Glamour is about feeling good in your own skin.
        —ZOE SALDANA, ACTRESS

But glamour's magic (literal and figurative) is its availability to anyone—not just rich men and peacocks. This may be why it became associated with femininity and women—and was diminished by that association. In being accessible to anyone, it becomes a tool of potential artifice—and this has long been a source of fear for men: older women might pretend to seem young, ugly women might pretend to be beautiful, poor women might pretend to be wealthy, and in so doing "trap" a man falsely. The word is rooted in this idea—it comes, by many accounts, from the Scots word *glamyre*, itself from *gramarye*, meaning "magic" or "enchantment." To be glamorous is to cast a spell. And as we discuss in the chapter on embracing your witchy ways, the ability to cast a spell and work magic has long been one of the more disparaged feminine powers.

DID YOU KNOW? The word "glamour" is close to—and, according to some etymologists, derived from—the word "grammar," which doesn't, in its original form, refer to your ability to diagram a sentence. "Grammar" originally referred to forms of learning—especially occult learning. Magic!

As a tool, however, glamour is extraordinarily powerful. Not just because of what it signals—it isn't necessarily about having the status bag or fancy car that announces, "I have money"—but because of how it can make you feel. For some women, it's

---

I'm not the type of person that needs to be all glammed up. I think femininity is being glammed up. I'm dressed up, I got my makeup, I've got my hair done to feel good. Some people say look good, feel good. Look good, feel good is not me. I think I am much more about what makes me feel good. People make me feel good. How I look doesn't make me feel good.
        —JULIE FOUDY, OLYMPIC SOCCER ICON AND JOURNALIST, ESPN

I don't think I could live without hair, makeup, and styling, let alone be the performer I am. I am a glamour girl through and through. I believe in the glamorous life, and I live one.
        —LADY GAGA, SINGER AND SONGWRITER

a kickass pair of heels or the perfect red lipstick. For others, it might be motorcycle boots and a great haircut. Some of the greatest icons of glamour—Greta Garbo, for example, or Jackie Kennedy—were very restrained in their style, but glamorous nonetheless, because it signaled extraordinary confidence. Did they always feel confident? Probably not. But they presented and carried themselves in a way that took that question right off the table. And any woman who has gotten through a difficult meeting or high-stakes interview or nerve-wracking date through the power of great hair or perfect lipstick can tell you, if you style yourself confident, the feeling will follow.

Entrepreneur Courtney Nichols Gould frames it nicely:

> What I really realized is I am not blow-out-your-hair and, wear makeup . . . it's not me. However, that doesn't mean I don't think of myself as sexy. It's just my style is not to have my nails done. It's just not my jam. I used to carry a lot of resentment on being female because I didn't like the fact that I was expected to do those things. So, part of it was I'm not going to do this because I don't want to be appealing. Then it evolved into, because my intention is to not have my appearance as part of the conversation, then the next phase of screw you, I don't want to do this because I don't feel like I should have to. You don't have to. That is part of me too, which is I want to do it because it's a joyful expression and it's fun to do, but I don't want to do it because it's expected. So, to me, glamorous is when you want to be glamorous. Not because you're expected to be.

Sometimes I like my ripped army pants, Birkenstocks, and bandana, because that's what I feel like that day. And that's the kind of energy that I'm in that day. And then, I can go out, and I can wear something that's skintight, super high heels, super high platforms, whatever I want, you know what I mean? Why are there not thirty-one flavors of sexy? Because I might feel really sexy in pajama bottoms and a ripped T-shirt and no makeup.

—JENNIFER GREY, ACTRESS

I believe in glamour. I am in favor of a little vanity. I don't rely on just my genes.

—IMAN, MODEL

In other words, glamour can be about dressing up to play a part, expressing a hidden part of yourself, or acting out a fantasy. Or it can be a natural expression of one's authentic style. In any case, we say, glam it up—fearlessly!

HOW TO BE GLAMOROUS

Find the thing that makes you feel great—powerful, in control, good about yourself. Maybe it's a piece of clothing, or makeup, or a great hairstyle. Maybe it's something that nobody can see—lingerie or your dad's pocket watch tucked into your bag. Maybe it's something that you do: a morning run or meditation. The important thing is that it makes you feel strong, such that you're able to carry yourself with the confidence of a peacock!

Do one thing every day to bring flair into your life. Be indulgent. Buy an outrageous bouquet of flowers. Order a very dry martini. Get the expensive chocolates. Flounce. Who's the most glamorous woman you know or know of? Ask yourself, What would she do (when ordering lunch, buying new sheets, asking for a raise, making a toast)?

Embrace the idea that superficial things—adornments and the like—can have meaning and significance and power. Sure, it's easy to disdain lipstick and manicures as mere enhancements of our outward appearance. But if they make you feel powerful, who cares? They have a deeper power. "Glamour" comes from an archaic word for magic for a reason—it's illusion, sure, but it's illusion with effect. It can make things happen. It puts you in control of your environment—it helps you control how people see you. Sephora is taking on a whole new light, isn't it?

The power suit—usually a pantsuit—is an iconic image in the history of women's empowerment. It's the shoulder pads of Melanie Griffith in *Working Girl*, the power blazers and big hair of the 1980s, the women's-cut menswear showcased by the first generation of supermodels. As Cindy Crawford told us, these things were a kind of armor: "When you look back at the fashion of the eighties, women were wearing suits that look exactly like men's suits, with the ties. Then they started the shoulder pads and the high heels and the hair up to there. That was like our armor, it was like power, being the glamazon. We look back now, we see the ridiculousness of it, but you understand where it came from— women trying to find their place in the workforce."

But is the power suit really an artifact of the past? Many of the women we spoke with brought it up explicitly as a uniform that they thought they had to adopt if they were going to not only succeed but find acceptance in a man's world. Christine Simmons said, "Early on in my career I was in that horrible pantsuit. You know what I mean. The pantsuit. I felt that I had to be in this pantsuit, and I couldn't have any style or femininity to it. By definition, the power suit was this really manly suit—and that meant I had to work in other ways to express my femininity. I had to use my charm and my wit instead."

And then, of course, there was Hillary Clinton. Her signature pantsuits became the emblem of a movement in the run-up to the 2016 presidential election: they

continues

continued

represented what it looks like to be a woman trying to compete in the field of leadership. The Facebook group Pantsuit Nation exploded in membership because so many women identified with that and wanted to reclaim the pantsuit as symbolic of their hard work and accomplishment and of the struggle to have those recognized. The pantsuit, then, became a kind of symbol for the struggle. Did it become a power suit again through that struggle? We think that's up to you. Power suit, power jeans, or power tutu—we need to define our power suits for ourselves.

—POWER SUIT NATION

CHAPTER 14

SHOW YOUR WEAKNESS

Vulnerability is the birthplace of innovation, creativity, and change.

—Brené Brown,
RESEARCHER, AUTHOR

We've talked a lot about how the traits and behaviors associated with femininity have long been characterized as weak. The problem, as we've seen, is that weakness is almost always framed as a bad thing. And so many of us have avoided weakness like the plague, working hard to be—and be seen as—strong, competent, and powerful. And we haven't had much choice, have we? We've had to do this to compete in a man's world.

But is weakness always a bad thing?

What others call weakness, we want to look at as openness. We believe that, for women, connecting to this openness means confronting all of the ingrained, socially conditioned biases against weakness in general. So many of those biases are rooted in the association of weakness with femininity—and as we've been saying all along, we want to turn those ideas on their head. We want to assert that what is often called weak is actually powerful.

AMY'S STORY

I have an amazing healer and bodyworker in New York City, Edan Harari, LMT, OMT. In a recent session, he talked about how when someone is upset, emotional, or overwhelmed, the best thing you can do is give him or her a big, strong hug and hold that person. It's a form of compression. I've always known that the hug is the solution to most problems—now I know there may be a scientific reason why.

I started thinking about femininity in part because I felt conflicted. I am a sensitive, vulnerable, gentle being on the inside and sometimes, mostly at work, bring my strength, toughness, and assertiveness. So many times these more masculine qualities are useful and practical. There's no way I could run a business without them. In fact, in thinking more about femininity, I see where I can effectively and purposefully allow those qualities to lead.

That said, through this process and as a result of experiences in my last few relationships, I know more clearly than ever what I'm looking for in a romantic partner.

I want to be taken care of.

Saying that out loud almost makes me cringe. But it's true. It's not about being financially taken care of. It's not about wanting someone else to complete me. In fact, it's not about *needing* to be taken care of. It's about *wanting* to be taken care of. And *allowing* myself to be taken care of. It's all about the hug!

I've dated men who have cherished me, looked after me, cared for me, and known the power of the hug—and it rocked my world. I know it may seem like a pretty typical thing to hope for in a partner, but for me, that feeling was new. I hadn't allowed myself to want that. Maybe it's the strong woman in me. I felt like it was wrong and weak to be a progressive and powerful woman in the workplace and still want a man to take care of me.

> But now I realize that's actually strength. To recognize and acknowledge what feels good and what I need. And not to be ashamed of it.

One form of weakness has already been culturally reframed. Brené Brown has done the groundbreaking work of showing that emotional vulnerability makes us human and that tapping into it is important, even necessary, in cultivating our well-being. Her widely shared and celebrated work (her TED talk on vulnerability is one of the most viewed in the history of the program) has given us a different cultural lens through which to view certain practices of emotional openness.

Brown shows that emotional vulnerability is not distinctly feminine—it's fundamentally human, inasmuch as it reflects the real practice at its core: the practice of authenticity, in the sense of exposing your real, authentic self rather than protecting it behind contrived identities. And authenticity is one of our most enduring and celebrated human values: philosophers and theologians from the earliest times have derided sham and artifice and urged thinking people to strive for honesty and authenticity. (Again, we can look to the Judeo-Christian origin story for clear evidence of how far back this goes: the first sign that Adam and Eve have sinned is that they hide themselves behind the—admittedly flimsy—protective cover of fig leaves.)

We used the word "people" just now, but, frankly, that's not entirely accurate. Philosophers and theologians (and poets and artists) have celebrated authenticity for millennia—but they've celebrated it in men. Women, on the other hand, have more often been associated with artifice and concealment—literally, figuratively, and sometimes conflictually: women have long been expected to conceal themselves within the private sphere, then criticized for hiding their true selves. They've long been seen as both caged and cagey! (See Chapter 13 on glamour and

but she was such a man. She was impenetrable—Nichols was psychologically astute to make her furniture and clothes so feminine, when in truth she was just faking it. Those were only external things; internally, she was totally cut off from her true self. You can't be penetrable unless you're vulnerable, and we grew up thinking it was unsafe to be vulnerable. Vulnerability was a girl thing. And we had outgrown it. Oh, God.

—MARIANNE WILLIAMSON, SPIRITUAL TEACHER, AUTHOR, AND LECTURER

You get to a stage in life where you realize that you need to be vulnerable in your relationship. I can be as strong as I want to and work. I can be as tough as I need to because I may not have the same advantages that my male counterpart may have, or even my white female counterpart or my nonminority counterpart may have. I may not have those same luxuries and the same excuses and built-in cushion. So I go in tough and strong and realize that I just don't get that second chance. But then when I go home, I need to be able to turn that all off. I need to take off my armor, and be a woman and lean into my vulnerability and

Chapter 15 on seduction for more about what this has looked like historically.)

But weakness more broadly has always been associated with women to the extent that the term "womanly" has, at various times in history, been used as a synonym for weakness. (To say nothing of "girl"! How often have you heard the phrase "like a girl" used as an insult? To run, throw, or fight like a girl is to do those things weakly, which is to say badly.) That use of "weak" points directly to a lack of strength or skill. Another closely related use relates to dependency or need: to lack strength or skill such that you must rely on the support of another. Yet another variation pertains to the lack of a particular strength: strength of will or the ability to resist (especially in the context of temptation—again, see the story of Eve in the garden). When we think of feminine weakness or of weakness in its most negative light, we usually think of these perceived weaknesses—the lack of strength, self-sufficiency, and will.

But leaning into those "feminine" weaknesses has its own unique and forceful power.

Consider weakness as lack of strength or skill. Knowing and being comfortable with your weaknesses can be extraordinarily powerful. Think about how much wasted time and energy gets channeled into futile endeavors by people who don't know (or acknowledge) their own weaknesses. Conversely, think about how efficient it is to ask for help with or delegate activities that you're not particularly good at. Even physical weakness has its strengths because asking for help has power. Acknowledging our weakness makes space for others to help us, to take care of us, to support us. And that dynamic, in turn, creates closeness and connectivity. Studies show that letting people help you actually makes them feel good. Acts of kindness and prosocial behavior in general contribute to a measurable happiness "boost" that actually exceeds the one you get when you do kind things for yourself. A 2016 study showed that practicing kindness toward others conduces more to "psychological flourishing" than doing nice things for yourself.

What about strength of will? Sure, willpower is great, but anybody who has tried to power through a restrictive diet or quit a vice through force of will can tell you that this strategy for overcoming anything is overrated. On the contrary, most current research on addressing addiction (or dieting, or any other endeavor that requires restricting our desires) tells us that admitting the limits of our willpower is the most important first step. Admitting weakness—acknowledging and embracing it as part and parcel of who we are—is crucial to cultivating strength.

And if you've learned nothing else from this book so far, you have probably learned this: any feminine trait associated with Eve is probably an actual superpower. And who's the most famous "tempted" human in history?

Right.

HOW TO OWN WEAKNESS

Do an inventory of the things that you're not good at or don't like doing. Those are your weaknesses. Give yourself permission to admit those—and then to say no to anything that falls into those categories or to ask for help with them. You can let go of responsibility for those things! Isn't that freeing?

Let others support you. Next time someone asks you if they can hold a door open or assist you in some way, say yes. Even if you don't actually need the help. Try this with different people and circumstances. See how it feels and how it impacts your relationships.

Ask others to support you. Pay attention to what your family, friends, and colleagues are good at and celebrate them for those things! It's flattering to be asked to do something that you're good at, so flatter people by asking them.

If you really need or depend on people, let them know. Say, "I couldn't do this without you" or "I couldn't *be* this without you." Real strength is shared. Let the people you depend on know that they're part of your team and that you're stronger together.

I'm not conscious of my femininity, because my femininity is already part of who I am. What I am conscious of, every minute, is the kind of person I want to be. I am conscious of acting in kindness, being empathetic, remaining grateful—the things the strain and stress of everyday life can sometimes let us forget. My focus—what lives in my consciousness when I raise my head off the pillow—is on how I want to show up in the world.

—SELA WARD, ACTRESS

CHAPTER 15

BE SEDUCTIVE

Most virtue is a demand for greater seduction.

—Natalie Clifford Barney,
American playwright

Seductiveness is arguably the ultimate feminine characteristic—or at least the oldest. Eve, after all, is often characterized as the first seductress, tempting Adam with the apple and triggering their expulsion from the garden. Bible literalists might consider this a bad thing, but consider this: the feminine practice of seduction, it could be said, was foundational to humanity's movement from ignorance to advancement. If Eve hadn't gotten us out of that garden, we might still be there, naked and lacking appletinis.

CATHERINE'S STORY

The heart of seduction, Jean Baudrillard once said, is challenge rather than desire. I learned the truth of this in a context that had nothing to do with sex or romance.

One of my professors in grad school was notably reserved in manner—a man of few words. This wasn't in itself unusual—academia attracts introverts—but it was striking in certain moments common to the academic environment. In symposia or panel discussions, in departmental committee meetings, in any situation wherein you would otherwise find a cacophony of voices fighting for the last word, he would be silent. Although clearly listening and thinking, he would say nothing. Until, invariably—and it really was invariable—all attention turned to him. By sitting back in his chair—by not fighting to be heard—he stood out, and his silence became a challenge. Why wasn't he saying anything? What was he thinking? The moderator of the panel or the chair of the meeting would lean in and ask him for his opinion or his input, which would all of a sudden seem intensely important—and authoritative. By withholding his contribution, he made it seem all the more important. When he finally spoke, everyone listened intently. They would literally lean in to hear him.

It wasn't until Amy and I were having early conversations about this book that I really understood that this withholding posture was maybe the purest form of seduction, the kind usually framed as feminine. That a man had most fully demonstrated this to me only underscored it's a power, one that only gets problematized when it's in women's hands.

It's a feminine power that we need to unproblematize.

The Bible, of course, is littered with seductive women who are characterized as sinful. Jezebel, Delilah, Salome: they seduce men and turn them from God, sometimes causing the downfall of nations in the process. And they're all over literature and culture, from ancient works like *The Odyssey*, through fairy tales and Shakespeare's plays, to films like *Basic Instinct* and *Cruel Intentions* (which is based on a famous work on seduction, *Les Liaisons Dangereuses*) and TV series like *The Vampire Diaries*. The temptress, seductress, or vamp is usually a strong character whose power seems almost supernatural (we talk more about this in the chapter on witchy ways). She's forceful, attractive, and undeniably compelling. Even Taylor Swift, whose brand leverages "good girl" stereotypes to maximum effect, can't resist playing the vamp in some of her songs ("Blank Space" is a vamp power song if there ever was one).

But the seductive female character—like feminine seductiveness in general—usually takes on, at the end of the day, a strongly negative cast. The vamp, after all, almost never has a happy ending: she ends up foiled, spurned, or (too often) dead. Male heroes escape her grasp, and "good girl" heroines prevail because of their purer virtue. Temptresses aren't to be trusted: they deal in cunning and illusion and strive to turn human weakness (male weakness) to their advantage. They're female tricksters, and nobody likes to be tricked.

. . . .

DID YOU KNOW? The word "seduce" stems from Latin and means literally "to lead away"—hence its early use to mean "to persuade." The sexual connotation of the term didn't become common until the Middle Ages.

. . . .

Male seducers don't get the same treatment, of course. Sure, they're often characterized as dangerous, but they're dangerous in an exciting, compelling way. The "devilish" rogue, an attractive, even lovable character, sometimes gets converted to good (usually by a pure-of-heart heroine), but even if not, he still sits somewhere on the "hero" spectrum as an "antihero" who, with a little work, could (or inevitably will) become fully heroic. Often, there's no ambiguity at all: the seductive rogue is the hero, and his roguishness is part and parcel of his heroism (Tony Stark, aka Iron Man, is a classic superhero example of this).

And they're everywhere in real life. Take away the movie-set glamour of "seduction" as a cultural idea, and you find real seducers at the top of every field. Business, politics, media—success

The seduction of passivity, patience, and vulnerability [is powerful]. That's what I teach women. Do it his way, unless you have to call the police, a doctor, or a lawyer. Do it his way, even if you think it's smarter some other way. That is seductive, because they [men] feel powerful. We feel cared for, because that's what they do in response.

—PAT ALLEN, PhD

in many fields requires an ability to attract people to your ideas and get them to do what you want. That's a kind of seduction, though it's not always called seduction—with men, it's more usually called charm, charisma, or magnetism. It's not sexual, but it nonetheless draws upon human desire.

And it's extraordinarily powerful. The ability to attract and influence other people is arguably one of the most forceful powers that a human being can have. And seduction is not manipulative (although it's often characterized as such when women are doing it): its power lies in inspiring people to want what you want. That's important: real, powerful seduction isn't about tricking people or manipulating them; it's about drawing them in, convincing them, and inspiring them. It involves influence and inspiration at their most nuanced, sophisticated, and effective.

And it's no less powerful in its feminine form—arguably, it's even more powerful because it is nuanced, purposeful, and careful. Because seductiveness as a feminine power is, and has always been, so culturally freighted—and sometimes dangerous— women have had to adapt their powers of influence to their most subtle forms. The danger can't be understated: the historic demonizing (sometimes literal) of female seductive powers reflects real and long-standing fear of them, fear that has at times been channeled in terrible directions. But claiming feminine power means resisting historic oppressions of those powers—it's just a matter of claiming them purposefully and thoughtfully.

That means embracing your seductive powers as positive powers of influence rather than illusion: "seduction" should never be a matter of leveraging false promises or deceit. And positivity is key: only use your powers of influence for good. Remember the examples from Catherine's story: the power of seductive influence is that it draws people to you willingly, even enthusiastically. It's magnetic and needn't involve any trickery whatsoever. It's really just a higher-order practice of self-confidence: if you are confident of your own magnetism and comport yourself accordingly, you'll manifest it—and that will draw people to you.

That's a pretty remarkable power.

USE YOUR SEDUCTIVE TOOLS

Confidence, confidence, confidence. Seductive people know that they have something that other people want to access—they own that. Figure out your most desirable traits. Do they include your intellect? Your business sense? Your charm? Your great taste? Cultivate your confidence in those. Do something each day that uses your special talents so that your muscle memory for feeling confident in them is strong.

Sit back. Seduction is all about drawing people to you—and sometimes that means sitting back and letting them come to you. It also means being willing to forgo attention—seduction is sometimes about withholding, and that requires a willingness to be sparing about how much you share your best qualities and talents. Practice purposeful withholding: choose to not lean into a conversation sometimes, especially when it involves lots of noisy, competing voices. Be willing to let people ask you for your opinion.

Be subtle. Identify powerful moments to quietly or implicitly assert how awesome you are—rather than wearing it on your sleeve. Let people discover for themselves that you have many extraordinary talents. This isn't about mastering the art of the humblebrag or knowing the right moment to let it slip that you went to college in the Boston area—that's mostly just annoying. It's about letting your amazingness speak for itself.

If you want a certain kind of attention, you want to cultivate a certain energy, cultivate it. Use it. And see how that feels.

—JENNIFER GREY, ACTRESS

It is not enough to conquer; one must learn to seduce.

—VOLTAIRE, FRENCH WRITER

I think right now it's so essential to find the beacons of femininity who have been in those traditional male domains to help define what it is to be feminine, to own femininity. Then I think it's the same thing with men too. I think that men in a way don't know how to deal with femininity because no one's taught them. All they're doing is a lot of them are acting defensively instead of embracing it. There is a sense of being threatened because they don't know what role they're supposed to play then.

The question, though, is how do we deal with that?

—SARAH BROKAW, THERAPIST AND COACH

CHAPTER 16

UNLEASH YOUR
WILD WOMAN

As a woman lives them, she will understand more and more of
these interior feminine rhythms, among them the rhythms of
creativity, or birthing psychic babies and perhaps also human
ones, the rhythms of solitude, of play, of rest, of sexuality, and
of the hunt.

—Clarissa Pinkola Estés,
*Women Who Run with the Wolves:
Myths and Stories of the Wild Woman Archetype*

When was the last time you felt out of control? Too emotional?
Too needy? Too sensitive? Hormonal? Not on top of every
single one of the bazillion things you're supposed to be handling?
Things slipping through the cracks? Did someone say, "You're out
of control" or "You're losing it"—or did you just say those things
to yourself? Women take a lot of criticism for a tendency to lose
control—or not to have it in the first place. We're told we're too
emotional, or too needy, or too obsessed with love; that we're not
rational enough, not strong enough; that we lack the self-control to
be trusted with positions of power.

But the stereotypes around women and control aren't always consistent. For example, women can excel at being in control (see Chapter 17)—but they are also great at supporting someone else's taking

the reins. Not being in control and sometimes actively giving it up—giving in to emotion, love, or weakness or ceding control over situations and circumstances to other people or maybe even fate—has a lot of benefits. Relinquishing control can be extraordinarily powerful. Letting go and going wild can, sometimes, be the most powerful thing you can do.

AMY'S STORY

In my late twenties, I traveled to northern Spain with Jeff, my boyfriend at the time. We had different traveling styles—I was a planner and liked to book hotels (optimally, nice ones) in advance (not much has changed). He preferred to travel more spontaneously (a higher-end, backpack-free version of backpacking). We agreed as we were planning the trip that we would divide the itinerary between half planned/reserved, half unplanned/unreserved. That worked for both of us. A good compromise.

One of our stops during the spontaneous part of our trip was The Pyrenees—an amazing *parador* (government-owned hotel) in the mountains—in the middle of nowhere. We drove on a long, winding road into the night to get there, arriving just in time to eat some dinner and go to bed. It was insanely dark—we couldn't see a thing.

We woke up to the tallest and most beautiful mountains I had ever seen—we were deep in the Pyrenees with nothing else around. Jeff arranged for a hike with the concierge—I couldn't understand any of the details because they were speaking Spanish and looking at a map, neither of which made sense to me. We grabbed our bagged lunches and off we went.

This was supposed to be a five-hour hike. It was more like eight hours. Six hours in, we were almost out of water, and it was windy and intense. We knew we only had a couple more hours of light. The map included a strange dotted line as part of the path down. Of course I had no idea what it meant; neither did Jeff. We ran into an English-speaking mountain man (the only human we saw all day), who said we were headed toward "the chains." Note: avoiding any sort of rock climbing was my only request pre-hike.

Finally, after the sixth hour, we came up to "the chains," a fifteen-foot rock wall with chains that we were supposed to climb down. I sat at the top of the wall and cried. Hysterically.

Eventually I climbed down. And took lots of pictures of me at the bottom of the chains—wearing a huge smile on my face.

You were once wild here. Don't let them tame you.

—Isadora Duncan, dancer

We've explored the power of letting go a little bit in other chapters, but there's a bigger picture here that's worth digging into because liberation itself is powerful. And although freedom and independence—the cornerstones of liberation—are usually framed as masculine values, a certain kind of freedom and independence is more usually framed as feminine. We're thinking of free-spiritedness—that is, the condition and experience of not caring or worrying about social expectations. We're talking about freeing our spirits from the constraints of rationality and social norms to explore and play and indulge in our own movements and impulses. And not feeling guilty about that total loss of control.

Being free-spirited is a kind of flow state: a state of being in which you figuratively "go with the flow"—the flow of your intuition, or nature, or whatever force you believe moves the universe. It's wildly powerful—and it's uniquely feminine (at least it's long been characterized that way).

As we've already seen, throughout history, women have been perceived as irrational. Wild, untamable women are an archetype that goes back to our earliest stories. Often that archetype is explicitly associated with nature. Consider the spirited goddesses of the Earth and the seasons. Homer's hymn to Demeter is his only poem about a female goddess—and it's entirely about the time that she overwhelmed the world with an explosion of emotion and in the process created the four seasons. Nature itself is associated with the feminine—we refer to Mother Nature, after all, not Father Nature. So is Fortune—the unknowable whims of the universe—which is always characterized as a lady. (Niccolò Machiavelli said, "Fortune is a woman." And because she is a woman, she cannot be predicted or controlled. Likewise Friedrich Nietzsche wrote, "What inspires respect for woman, and often enough even fear, is her nature.")

Some of this is rooted in long-standing (male) fears about female disobedience. So much of the architecture of (most) societies has long depended on women's compliance—their willingness to stay in their proper place (the home and other domestic spaces) and do the work assigned to them (child-rearing, caregiving, household management). And so "disobedient" women who follow their own desires and reject social convention have long been deemed "wild" in the most negative sense. They are, in this view, literally antisocial: they are indulging their animal natures rather than conforming to the norms of civilized society.

Such wildness, of course, also rejects the norms of the good girl. And despite the many benefits to embracing those norms (see Chapter 11), there are also powerful reasons to—at least sometimes—ignore them. Clarissa Pinkola Estés explains this beautifully in *Women Who Run with the Wolves*:

> While it is useful to make bridges even to those groups one does not belong to, and it is important to try to be kind, it is also imperative to not strive too hard, to not believe too deeply that if one acts just right, if one manages to tie down all the itches and twitches of the wildish *criatura*, that one can actually pass for a nice, restrained, subdued, and demure lady-woman. It is that kind of

acting, that kind of ego-wish to belong at all costs, that knocks out the Wild Woman connection to the psyche. Then instead of a vital woman you have a nice woman who is de-clawed. Then you have a well-behaved, well-meaning, nervous woman, panting to be good. No, it is better, more graceful, and far more soulful to just be what and as you are and let the other creatures be what they are too.

Connecting to our impulses toward wildness and unpredictability, to our ability to track with the mysterious movements of nature and the universe, to our capacity to embrace uncertainty and "go with the flow" is, in other words, a means of connecting to our natural selves. And even if you don't buy that there's anything naturally feminine about this, it's hard to dispute the power of connecting to your vitality and putting a high value on your emotional and spiritual freedom. Moreover—and this is especially important for those of us who don't aspire to goddess-like levels of free-spiritedness—it makes us happy. Research has shown that connecting to the wild does meaningfully boost our psychological well-being. Even just embracing uncertainty brings pleasure to our lives, in part because it adds spice and color (as one author points out, "spoiler alerts" acknowledge that knowing what's going to happen in advance takes away the fun).[1]

Embracing uncertainty and "going with the flow" also puts us in touch with remarkable powers of creativity and learning. It allows us to experience things we wouldn't otherwise. It expands our experience and capacity for exploration. Think about traveling in a foreign land and losing your way: stressful and uneasy moments aside (assuming you prefer to be in control), getting lost may end up among your most memorable experiences—you couldn't have planned (or controlled) it if you tried.

Letting go is a path to growth. Who knew?!

LET GO AND BE WILD

Do something that scares you every day. Push yourself to the limit. Know that it's going to be uncomfortable. Embrace the experience. Be emotional and overwhelmed. Take it all in.

Don't resist. Our instinct may be to tense up and constrict when we're feeling that loss of control. Try relaxing physically and emotionally and see what happens. Maybe you'll experience both the process and the outcome in a more positive way.

Let nature fuel your flow. Spend time in nature. Experience the elements (go for a run in the rain). Feel the power of this ultimate mother (Earth). Swim in the ocean and feel the power of the waves—dangerous yet exhilarating. Let nature test and unleash you.

Surround yourself with those who love you when you lose it. Know that it's OK to have moments when you're out of control (emotionally or otherwise). Find people who allow and embrace this. Maybe they know just when to give you the bear hug that allows you to rebalance.

Our Favorite Wild Women:

Annie Oakley
Elizabeth Gilbert
Cheryl Strayed
Yoko Ono
Demeter

For me, femininity has positive connotations. What comes to mind as soon as I hear that word is womanly power. Inherent in that is softness, but also strength. Someone who exudes or displays femininity needs to possess confidence or else they wouldn't be able to fully inhabit the most identifiable attributes of our gender. I kind of envy women who can do that organically because I have probably suppressed those qualities to some degree.

—MICHELE PROMAULAYKO,
EDITOR IN CHIEF, *COSMOPOLITAN*

CHAPTER 17

BE CONTROLLING

Let me take a minute to say that I love bossy women. Some people hate the word, and I understand how "bossy" can seem like a shitty way to describe a woman with a determined point of view, but for me, a bossy woman is someone to search out and celebrate. A bossy woman is someone who cares and commits and is a natural leader.

—Amy Poehler, actress

In Chapter 10 we talk about surrender and letting go, and that was, in some ways, a tough chapter for both of us to write. Perhaps it was a tough chapter for you to read too. You may have been thinking that it's completely impossible to give up control in certain areas of your life. You have so much to do and so many things to manage—work, the household, parenting. If you don't keep on top of certain things, disaster may ensue! The stakes are just too high for us to give up control in so many areas of our lives.

And despite historically lacking political or social power, women have, in fact, long been expected to exercise powers of control in certain domains. There's good reason why women are often characterized as organizers—as detail oriented and uniquely able to keep things on track—and why they are so often expected to function as project managers (whether they get credit for this or not). Who organized your company's last holiday party? We don't have to guess—it was almost certainly a woman.

Women have typically managed households from the very beginning. Even Aristotle recognized that women needed some power in the private domain: Who else would run the home while men did the important public work of being citizens and wealth earners?

AMY'S STORY

I have been described as strong and bossy from a young age by certain family members who shall remain nameless. They rarely mean it as a compliment. I know that as much as they make fun of me and joke about it, they appreciate and respect my strength, especially when it doesn't conflict with them in any way.

I was shy in high school. I definitely didn't feel like the boss.

I was the head counselor at John Gardiner's Tennis Ranch—I think because I was a good organizer and able to multitask and keep track of dozens of camper problems at the same time.

I was the captain of my tennis team, but as I recall, this was because I was playing number one singles and overall a good team player, not because I was leading or driving the team.

Now, at my company, I'm officially the boss. As much as I've always wanted to have my own business and take charge of my own destiny, I find many aspects of running a business challenging.

At the top of that list: being the boss.

I'm still a good project manager, multitasker, and problem solver. I guess those are important qualities for a boss. I make the final decisions. I break hard news to people and have the tough conversations. I have to say no to my employees, even when that's unpopular and I might prefer to say yes.

I do my best to run my business with integrity, grace, kindness, and empathy. I'm sure that on some days my employees or clients don't see it that way. That's all part of being the boss.

In the end, being the boss taps into your gifts, your leadership skills, and your ability to keep things moving and on track. Some days you may seem bossy or controlling; other days, you may be seen as a good leader.

What will tomorrow bring?

Women have cultivated organizational skills over millennia and put them to good use in a variety of ways: in addition to managing households (no small thing!), we've also organized and managed entire social movements (we wouldn't have gotten the vote if we hadn't been excellent organizers). But there's an irony to the feminine role of getting things done: when we're leaning into our managerial tendencies and running the show, we're all too likely to hear that we're being controlling or bossy. And whereas, when applied to a man, this is a compliment, when applied to a woman, it's not.

Stories, often tragicomic, about controlling women who get in men's way litter history, myth, and folklore. What is a shrew or harpy, battle axe or bitch other than a woman who is exerting control? Shakespeare mastered this characterization. He devotes his *The Taming of the Shrew* entirely to confronting the feminine archetype of the difficult woman (who appears in some form or another in many of his other plays) and "taming" her. He borrowed the archetype from folklore predating his work by centuries, and it has surfaced time and again since (think of *Kiss Me Kate* to *10 Things I Hate About You*). The shrew is transgressive—she breaks the feminine code of subservience to men—but the persistence of this archetype (and the depth of its history) shows that her resistance and refusal to bow are deeply feminine. (Eve, the first woman of Judeo-Christianity, after all, refused to be subservient!)

· ·

DID YOU KNOW? The word "shrew" derives from the Middle English *shrewe*, or scolding person. We'll stick with bossy, thanks.

· ·

This archetype is extraordinarily powerful, of course. Not because assertion of control and refusal to be dominated are perceived as powerful (and masculine) in our culture—although they are—but because feminine exercise of control outside designated feminine domains is considered bad behavior. It breaks long-standing, established social rules. It takes on the feminine stereotype of subservience and insists that a woman can reject it. It's an assertion of female independence as important and necessary. It's why a "bossy" girl stands out in a way that an assertive boy simply doesn't (and why boys never get called "bossy"). The bossy girl or woman is standing up not just for what she can control but for her very right to control. And that right has historically been contested because women and girls—despite the weight of responsibilities placed upon them—were for a very long time (most of human history) denied political rights of control (voting, for example, and ownership of property, etc.).

So, "bossiness," or assertion of control, by women and girls outside traditionally feminine spaces like home and family is often perceived as problematic. Think of some reactions to Hillary Clinton's run for presidency: How often was she characterized as "shrill"? Many saw her authoritativeness as wrong or discordant; many who said that they just didn't like her really meant that they were uncomfortable with a woman's asserting authority. When Donald Trump called her a "nasty woman," he didn't mean that she was unkind or impolite; he meant that she deviated from the norm. By laying claim to a position of public authority, she was pushing the limits of a long-standing social norm: women don't assert powers of control in the public sphere. If she wanted to control her household or a small private business, fine. The entire United States of America? Many couldn't accept that outcome, even though she was far more qualified than the man running against her.

At the same time, as a culture, we welcome feminine control in appropriate spaces—again, the household, the family, and domains that seem related to either, such as caregiving institutions (although, even here, "control" or management doesn't always translate to status; a hospital may be functionally run by female nurses and administrators, but the highest salaries and titles still disproportionately go to men) and human resources and business operations departments. Women now more frequently fill the role of chief operating officer (COO), in part because of what one writer called "the Sandberg effect," noting that Sheryl Sandberg's successful run as COO of Facebook seems to have set an aspiration for women.[1] But it's worth noting that the role of COO—especially next to a famous or charismatic male CEO—feels a little bit like the role of "wife": the COO, after all, does the boring, day-to-day stuff—the "hard, dirty, but important work that it takes to make a business run."[2] (This isn't necessarily a bad thing! We examine this further in Chapter 18 on embracing the supporting role.)

You might ask, So what? If women are welcomed in certain powerful "controlling" roles, shouldn't we embrace that? Absolutely. But we should also recognize that our talents for managing and controlling are really very valuable powers that we could and should embrace—and use—more openly. This is not to say that we should aim to compete with men in being unabashedly domineering; some modes of control are emphatically not positive or productive (the entirety of human history has demonstrated that amply). We are talking about purposeful control: taking responsibility, moving things forward, assuming

I started taking a positive ownership of being aggressive. I do have an opinion, and that makes me an intentional person who believes and is passionate about things. We're not taught how to properly confront people with both grace and accountability. It's either we let them slide by, doing x, y, and z, whatever it is, and we're like, "Oh, we're being graceful." We're giving them grace. They're allowed to do it—people are allowed to mess up. But true love requires grace and accountability.

—ALEXIS JONES, FOUNDER, I AM THAT GIRL

authority, leading in whatever capacity serves getting to the most positive possible result, be it a healthy family, a thriving business, or a robust democracy.

And this requires understanding what "controlling" really means and distinguishing between the kind of controlling that can get us into trouble—the kind that tries to control other people, that makes winning the priority—and the kind that is purposeful and productive—the kind that takes responsibility, moves things forward, and takes care of the family, community, or team. In other words—leadership.

This is important. Women have, throughout history, been strong and effective leaders. For most of history, they usually demonstrated this in the home, but in plenty of historical exceptions, women have proven themselves as leaders in the public domain (Joan of Arc, Boudica, Catherine the Great, Cleopatra—the list is long!). And although female leadership has not always reflected values or traits traditionally associated with femininity (Margaret Thatcher was called the Iron Lady for a reason), a number of traditionally feminine qualities do serve women's capacity for leadership in powerful ways—and we should celebrate them. Studies have shown, for example, that feminine practices of nurture and support can be powerful assets in leadership, as can powers of intuition (see Chapter 5), emotional intelligence (see Chapter 1), strong communication skills (see Chapters 4 and 6), empathy, compassion, strong social skills, and on and on. In fact, some studies show that these feminine qualities can be more effective than traditional male qualities when it comes to effective leadership.

Female leadership, in other words, doesn't just mean (shouldn't mean) women dressed in men's power suits. It means bringing our best qualities to the table when we're in control of anything—exercising our feminine powers in the most positive and productive ways. It also means modeling this as a new kind of leadership—in effect, expanding the traditional definitions of power and leadership to include feminine qualities long framed as weak or inappropriate for the public sphere. It means asserting that feminine models of leadership can be just as effective—in some cases, more effective—than the masculine ones that have dominated for most of human history.

If that's being controlling, let's do more of it.

CONTROLLING IN ACTION

Distinguish good controlling from bad controlling. Consider whether you are using your "skills" to get things done and make things happen or attempting to control another person or situation (beyond your control) in a way that's not serving a good end. Ask yourself why you're leaning into control in any given situation. Is it for a productive good? Or is it controlling for controlling's sake? The latter is just dominance and can get problematic. You want to lead because your leadership will make good things happen. Stick to that, and you'll truly be in your power.

Look at the fruits of your controlling nature. Take pride in your ability to make sh*t happen! Instead of feeling drained and exhausted by your never-ending to-do list, give yourself credit for completing tasks. Focus on the positive.

Don't shy away from being the boss. Own it. Assert it. Model it for other women—and for girls.

You can be the boss and be feminine at the same time. Feminine leadership has a long and fascinating history. If you're being called "bossy," you're probably, as entrepreneur Courtney Nichols Gould says, "just f*cking good." You're simply claiming your power, lady. If you're using it well, that's all that matters.

I think at the core of us, we're unifiers, right? I mean, we keep families together, we build communities, we build villages. It's the women who make the good decisions. We have good instincts. Again, it's not to say men don't do that, but on a whole, I'd have a lot more confidence right now if this world was being run by women. It's a fact.

—Julie Foudy, Olympic soccer icon and journalist, ESPN

That split between our feminine self and our feminist goals resulted in a terrible psychic tear. Over the last couple of decades, women have been trying to repair that breach, and I think in many ways we have. But doing so at times has been more difficult than you might expect. I remember feeling as though, in order to get into certain rooms of power or authority back then, I needed claws instead of finger nails. I had to claw my way into the room. But once I was in, I said, "Okay, I don't need the claws anymore"—and it wasn't so easy to take them off! The claws had become cemented onto my psyche; they'd become attitudinal habits. I had become the tough woman I thought I had to become. And maybe, in those days, I did.

—MARIANNE WILLIAMSON, SPIRITUAL TEACHER, AUTHOR, AND LECTURER

I was in a negotiation on behalf of a client, and I had to tear the other side apart a little bit. I thought they were being disingenuous, I caught them in some representations that weren't true, and I went after them. Look, I can even admit that I was kind of a raving bitch, but the situation called for it on behalf of this client, it really did. I don't think that at any point in time I lost a sense of who I was. Different contexts in the professional world call for different responses, and I'm not, at this point in my career, I am not afraid of anyone saying, "She's a bitch." It's worked for me. I'm finally at a place in my life where I own my success, and nobody's really handed me anything. It's all been earned. However I've been operating has gotten me to where I am, and I'm really happy with where I am, so I'm just going to keep doing what I've been doing.

—KAREN BRODKIN, EXECUTIVE VICE PRESIDENT,
CONTENT STRATEGY AND PARTNERSHIPS, IMG

The feminine is the way to leapfrog in our evolution, and the masculine is there to support that.

—DAWN CARTWRIGHT, TANTRIC VISIONARY

CHAPTER 18

EMBRACE THE
SUPPORTING ROLE

Helping others isn't a chore; it is one of the greatest gifts
there is.

—LIYA KEBEDE, ETHIOPIAN MODEL

Women have always been understood to stand—literally and
figuratively—behind men. With very few exceptions, they
have been positioned as secondary: Eve was made from Adam; Hera
was subservient to Zeus; Jackie Kennedy stood behind Jack. Their
place has traditionally been behind the scenes—in the domestic
realm, the private sphere, the home. Only very recently in human
history have women gained meaningful opportunities to lead. And
even though they still don't have as many leadership opportunities as
men, they continue to chase those they do have.

Seeing is believing when it comes to breaking barriers and achieving great things: if we've seen others do it, we know it's possible. We
continue to push the limits and strive for greatness—in some cases,
we attain it; in others, we come close (Hillary Clinton very nearly
shattered the ultimate glass ceiling). We know that we can shine at
the top. And as part of "competing in a man's world," some of us
have convinced ourselves that we need to fight our way there.

But who decided that's where we all want to be?

There's no better starting point than Michelle Obama in thinking about how number two can be powerful. With her grace, power, and poise, she didn't need to be front and center in order to make a huge impact. Michelle is the matriarch, the secret weapon, the muse. She actually seems presidential herself but walks alongside her husband with humility and pride. She doesn't need to have the loudest voice or the most prestigious title; yet she exudes power. As her husband Barack once said, "For the past 25 years, you've not only been my wife and the mother of my children, you've been my best friend. You took on a role you didn't ask for and you made it your own with grace, grit and style." He also acknowledges how critical she is: "Obviously I couldn't have done anything that I've done without Michelle. . . . [N]ot only has she been a great first lady, she is just my rock. I count on her in so many ways every single day."

Being someone's rock—how powerful is that?

The pursuit of hard power, the desire to run the show, isn't for everybody. If the primary message about female empowerment is that it requires the pursuit of hard power—dominance, leadership, rule—then where does that leave girls and women (and boys and men!) who don't want to dominate or be out in front? For some, remaining behind the scenes actually appeals more than standing in the spotlight or carrying the heaviest burden of responsibility. So, what if we celebrated the choice to stand back and be number two? Sure, we can always choose to strive to be number one—some of us are always going to want that. But what if we recognized the power in making the intentional choice *not* to seek the spot out in front and to lead from behind (or beside!) instead?

We talked a bit about this in Chapter 17 on being controlling—because being supportive or taking a supporting role doesn't necessarily mean giving up control. Some of the most powerful positions in business are deputy positions: the chief operating officer, for example, embodied for many by Sheryl Sandberg, is a tremendously powerful role in a large business; in American government, the secretary of state often plays second fiddle (a role that Hillary Clinton filled brilliantly in the Obama administration). And this isn't a new idea. Niccolò Machiavelli argued in his famous work of political strategy, *The Prince*, that real influence resides not in the crown but in counsel: the advisor's soft power, he says, is almost always more potent than the hard power of the prince. (Machiavelli also acknowledged, subtly, that this kind of power is often associated with women. His Caterina Sforza in *Discourses on Livy* and his Lucrezia in *La Mandragola* are arguably both examples of women who wield unexpected, behind-the-scenes influence through their feminine cleverness.)

And there's ample evidence of this in present-day research. Robert Kelley has pioneered work in the field he calls "followership," the study of social dynamics in the space around leaders, and has found many scenarios in which the influence of empowered followers (he distinguishes passive followers from what he calls "star followers") is at least as crucial to social and political outcomes as the actions of the leader. And business writers have been tracking the influence of deputies for a while now: the *Wall Street Journal*'s Sue Shellenbarger, for example, has pointed out that deputies have special access to the "corners of power" and to information without the pressure of being in the spotlight. She argues that if your psychological profile doesn't require the ego stroking and public credit that come with being number one, the number two slot may be for you.

And that describes many of us, women and men alike. Some of us do, sometimes, want to stand back, play a supporting role, and lead from behind—and that choice needn't represent a compromise of our power. In fact, we might say that it represents an embrace of a different and potentially transformative kind of power: the power of support, cooperation, and collaboration. What if we celebrated peer leadership, teamwork, and mutual support as much as we do individual leadership and control?

What a radically different world that could be.

someday, but I've had a blast helping realize other people's visions. Maybe that sounds to some like I'm selling myself short or "settling," but I find grace in the supporting role because you can't be a good number one if you don't have a killer number two.

—KRISTEN CASTREE, MARKETING EXECUTIVE

HOW THE SUPPORTING ROLE IS POWERFUL

Recognize the power of the deputy. Being number two doesn't mean giving up power: you simply wield a different kind of power. It's a supportive power—no less influential because it functions behind the scenes. Enjoy the access you have, the importance of your position, and the value you bring. Be proud of your role—and use it well.

Build trust. With your number one but also—and sometimes more crucially—with everyone else. Deputies often act as conduits between public leaders and their teams and other communities—and that works best when a healthy degree of trust runs in all directions.

Be a role model. The deputy's power resides, in part, in collaboration, cooperation, and support. It's an important alternative to "hard power" models of leadership: share your example as widely as you can so that others see it as a great option. Yes, you love being a deputy because you don't crave the spotlight, but you recognize you're setting an example so that new generations of ambitious young women (and men!) can see how powerful it is to be supportive rather than dominant.

My feeling is that my generation and many generations of women, we by nature spark community, and we work towards the greater good. To be respected by the man in business or even in our own home, we have to learn many, many more skill sets than the man ever has had to learn. I've had to learn to be a good student. I had to get good grades. I had to be a businesswoman. I had to support myself financially. I had to make my own dinner. Then I had to be a great mother, great wife. Those are all skill sets it has been expected of us to learn. I don't believe men have been expected to learn those kinds of skill sets. My practitioner says, "That's why women at this stage are at a much higher level of evolution than men."

—GEETA NOVOTNY, WORLD-CLASS
OPERA SINGER AND SINGING INSTRUCTOR

CHAPTER 19

SING AND DANCE

Oh Woman, come before us, before our eyes longing for beauty, and tired of the ugliness of civilization, come in simple tunics, letting us see the line and harmony of the body beneath, and dance for us. Dance us the sweetness of life. Give us again the sweetness and the beauty of the true dance, give us again the joy of seeing the simple unconscious pure body of a woman. Like a great call it has come, and women must hear it and answer it.

—ISADORA DUNCAN, DANCER

The association of dancing with women and femininity has deep roots, reaching back into antiquity and beyond. From cave paintings to Egyptian frescos, Indian statuettes, rock art, pottery shards, vases, and ancient Greek and Roman art, women figure prominently in the history of dance. In some cases, that history related to ritual; in others it related to celebration and community. Only relatively recently, in the scope of human history (over the last few hundred years), has it become a performative activity undertaken on the stage. Belly dancing has a long history as a type of folk dance, and some theorize that it was originally performed to strengthen women's abdominal muscles for childbirth. Today, women take belly and pole dancing classes for the physical workout and also to embrace their femininity and boost their self-esteem. It increases physical strength, confidence, and, of course, feminine power.

Singing, too, has a long-standing association with feminin-ity. From the lullaby of the mother, grandmother, or nanny to the poetry of the seductive chanteuse crooning to the melodies of her all-male band (and it is always an all-male band), the magic of the voice has long been connected to women (or, for what it's worth, feminine men—the castrati reflected the high value placed on the feminine high soprano). Aoidē, meaning "song" in ancient Greek, was one of the three original muses, the female embodiments of the arts, worshiped for their influ-ence over the richest parts of human culture.

AMY'S STORY

I haven't danced since I was a child. As a little girl, I took ballet, tap, jazz. I remember my uncle picking me up in my pink leotard and taking me for ice cream (it seems I began rewarding my workouts with food at a young age!). In junior high, I continued to take dance classes in school, danced (always as a supporting cast member) in school plays, and quickly realized I didn't have a career ahead in dance (my best friend in high school was a legit dancer, and my lack of skill became increasingly clear). That didn't stop me from continuing to take dance class with my mom in my high school years. I always loved it and am not sure why my dance classes stopped abruptly after high school.

At my company, we regularly do group workouts, each time choosing a new workout in a new place. We have a lot of fun trying new things together (boot camp on the beach, yoga, rebounding, boxing, and more), even if we're pushed outside our individual comfort zones. Last Jan-uary, one of the girls took us all to LA Dancefit, a West Los Angeles–based dance studio where the fabulous Ilyse Baker teaches a class called Dancinerate. We had a blast. While I personally felt fairly uncoordinated and my head was spinning, I loved it and told myself that I'd go back when I had the time.

That took a year. In January, interestingly at the same time as I was closely studying the feminine and we were developing the proposal for this book, I started taking dance class with Ilyse. Soon I was a regular and taking not only her class, which mixes genres (jazz, lyrical, hip-hop, etc.), but also Latin Hip-Hop, Zumba, you name it. I even performed as part of a "dance team" with my other favorite instructor, Kian Kirk. Talk about performing outside of my comfort zone.

While dancing does require focus and thinking (especially the choreography classes), after a lot of practice, I find that it has become a way of freeing and expressing myself. It has become a direct channel to my femininity.

Singing is speaking from the authentic place of our emotions. It opens up a lot of channels, energetic channels. It brings down the fight or flight. It works in your circulatory system, helps bring your central nervous system into balance, which helps us be better able to receive, really understand our intuition, and then once we're on that intuitive path and that purpose, we understand how to move through the signs. We take the signs, and we have trust in how to move through something.

—GEETA NOVOTNY, WORLD-CLASS OPERA SINGER AND SINGING INSTRUCTOR

The association of singing and dancing with femininity persists to the present day. There are male singers and dancers, of course, but when we think of singing and dancing as disciplines or pastimes, we tend to think of them as primarily for girls and women. It's the girls who sing aloud and sign up for dance class. And what's more stereotypically feminine than a ballerina?

DID YOU KNOW? Ballet can be traced back to Italian court festivals in the Middle Ages. At the time women often played the male parts, and the first celebrated ballerinas were born at the Paris Opera in late seventeenth-century France.

Movies from *My Fair Lady* to *Dirty Dancing* and *La La Land* tell stories of women evolving, growing up, finding themselves, and actualizing through singing and dancing. The rare film that addresses the male experience of song and dance tends to view it through the lens of challenged gender assumptions: *Billy Elliot* was a moving film because it told the story of one boy's passion for dance against the gender biases of his community. And how many movies have we seen in which the stereotypically female ballet student learns to let go of her inhibitions when she meets a rough-and-tumble male street dancer who refuses to follow the feminine rules of dance, despite his talent?

But whether you consider traditional forms of dance and song restrictive or liberating, or whether you love ballet and opera or street dancing and rap, all forms of song and dance unquestionably involve tapping into our innermost desires to move and use our voices. And there's real power in doing exactly that.

Singing and dancing allow us to let go, to share ourselves, to be truly in the moment. The freedom we experience from taking time for ourselves and letting ourselves go physically and emotionally is distinctly feminine. And as we all know, nothing is more attractive than when someone owns her movement and is confident in her body.

Dancing provides all sorts of physical benefits: it not only enhances flexibility and strength but also makes you aware of body parts you never knew existed and teaches you how to move them. Shake your hips, point your toes, cup your hands—the subtleties of dance moves and styles and reminders about the influences of classical dance combine with practice and experience to create a unique physical experience. It can be an act, it can be playful, it can be spontaneous; we can try new things and do a routine differently every time.

The same holds for singing. Singing is about self-expression and has the various nuances of style, tone, emotion, and finding your voice. This is such an important part of developing confidence and loving yourself. As opera singer and singing instructor Geeta Novotny says, singing is a pathway to authenticity. "Singing helps us find and keep our authentic voices revitalized;

making it more than just a tool we use to communicate, but also an instrument for healing, inspiration and creativity," she says. "Our voices are a gift to give and through singing we can thus learn to better integrate our empowered voices into our everyday lives."

Singing and dancing may feel uncomfortable at times—but that's okay. We gain power from pushing through our discomfort. Dancing or singing may feel challenging or embarrassing. All the better! We feel unparalleled satisfaction and relief after a new and sometimes dreaded experience—we know we did it! We feel more powerful as a result. But remember, too, that the power here doesn't derive from developing the ability to sing or dance perfectly or at a professional level. You're not preparing to perform; you're doing this to serve your own joy. It doesn't matter how you sound or what you look like. What matters is that you're doing it—and that it feels good. As Ilyse Baker says,

> Being a woman isn't always so easy as we all desire to look our best, feel sexy and confident and be "the total package" type of a woman. We wear so many hats at any given moment and "guilty as charged" put our needs on the back burner, only to fall into a rut with the regularly felt emotions of stress and overwhelm. Dance can allow us to step out of our comfort zones and just let go! Think of it as an hour of playing pretend. You can be anyone you want to be or look any way you want . . . then you literally become it! Just get out of your head and allow yourself to explore your movement to tell your personal story through your dance. With some good music and the right atmosphere, dance can enable us all to let our inner rock stars out. Dance movement is all about women finding that safe haven to put themselves first and enjoy their own personal journey. When you dance it is all about *you*! It is your personal time to feel sexy, sassy, and strong.

maybe feels more intimidating or stronger around me. I think getting more and more in touch with that we will have less and less of those situations. I think connecting with our voice and finding ways to hear our own voice, we will be better able to use our own voice.

—SHEL PINK,
FOUNDER,
SPARITUAL

Singing is just a feeling set to music.

—CARRIE UNDERWOOD,
SINGER AND
SONGWRITER

Dancing can be about finding a safe space to be free, sharing an intimate part of ourselves, unleashing a part of our personality that may not get out to play as often as we'd like. As a form of art and self-expression, singing and dancing can help us tap into something we might not be able to access regularly. Dance has been considered a feminine form of meditation, a way for women to access a flow state.

How fortunate that we can find our power through something so fun!

SOURCING POWER FROM DANCING, SINGING, AND SELF-EXPRESSION

Feel the emotion. When singing or dancing, allow yourself to attach to a particular feeling or emotion. Whatever it is—sadness, anger, seduction—roll with it. Allow this to push your dancing and singing to a new level.

Enjoy the release. Notice how you feel after you dance. Or after you sing. Lighter? More relaxed? Note: you can literally do this anytime and almost anywhere!

Remember, this is self-care. Carve out time for singing and/or dancing the same way you would your yoga class. These things don't require a formal lesson or class. Sing in the shower. Have a dance party with your daughter or your dog.

Push through the discomfort. You're putting yourself out there. You will trip and fall flat (literally). And that's OK. The liberation comes as a result of the hard work and on the other side of the pain.

Don't judge yourself. Don't get hung up on being "good." Remember, you're singing and dancing for you. You don't have to be stage ready; in fact, isn't it more fun to treat this as play? How does that saying go? "Dance [and sing!] like nobody's watching."

We are in the fluid, ambiguous time. I think for the first time people are defining femininity for themselves. Even in the feminist movement, it used to be, This is the way of the feminist movement, because they were very practical and straightforward in the things that we need to achieve—we need to have the right to vote, we need to have equal rights. And it ended up taking on a masculine perspective that was called not feminine. So now people get to own their femininity in all different kinds of ways. Lena Dunham is super outspoken about feminism to her and what it means and how it is a nonjudgmental place and that femininity means that everyone is doing their own thing and as long as everyone is empowered by it and not doing it for reasons outside of their own self, go for it. I think girls and women are owning their tomboy-ness, and that is feminine to them. Other girls are just fully owning their pink, bows and things like that. There is more pride in it, and it is not assumed. It's just like, I love pink bows and dresses and polka dots and anything pink. This has become an empowering ownership of that. I think it's changing not to any one way. But I think it is changing just that girls are starting to question how they define it for themselves and sort of owning that, and that becomes buckets of this kind of femininity.

—EMILY GREENER, COFOUNDER, I AM THAT GIRL

CHAPTER 20

BE ROMANTIC

Romance is the glamour which turns the dust of everyday life into a golden haze.

—Elinor Glyn,
British novelist

L ove stories are as old as storytelling itself. Whether in the form of poems, songs, odes, or tales, the earliest records of human language show that love has long been one of our obsessions. From Orpheus and Eurydice to Romeo and Juliet and beyond, through myth and religious text, fairy tale and folklore, love stories have driven art, literature, and music for millennia. Even the modern word "romance" is connected to story: it derives from the word for the vernacular language in which the chivalric tale, a form of love story, was told. Human beings have been in love with love for a very long time.

AMY'S STORY

My mom is and has always been a romantic. She looks at the world through rose-colored glasses. She sees the good in people, generally giving everyone the benefit of the doubt. She prefers to focus on the positive. She's constantly looking for magic and trying to find ways to make it herself. Nothing makes her happier than love stories with happy endings (and she's eagerly awaiting a happy ending to mine!).

So, you can imagine her devastation when her first marriage (to my dad) didn't work out. While they were very different individuals and, on top of that, had grown apart, the divorce, though not surprising, was still a shock to her system. It didn't fit with the happy and perfect life she had anticipated and was trying to create.

She was crushed. She cried. A lot. She couldn't imagine dating. She couldn't imagine starting all over again. That said, Jan Stanton is a *doer*. And as depressed as she was about the idea of dating again, she was more focused on starting a new life and moving forward. She was not going to wallow in the sadness.

She heard about a guy named Rick Holz. He had been the quarterback on the football team at Beverly Hills High (Los Angeles born and raised, like my mom). Tall, dark, and handsome (bizarrely, he looked quite a bit like my dad), he was a family man, and he was kind. This was all my mom needed to know. She began asking everyone she knew about Rick Holz and found a number of people with connections to him, some more legit than others. Many of these people offered (actually, more likely agreed) to put in a good word for her. (Nobody says no to Jan Stanton.)

Meanwhile, Rick Holz noticed the same name and description popping up repeatedly on the list of fix-ups he kept on his desk: Jan Stanton, pretty, petite, brunette. He called. And on their first date, she told him the story of the pursuit. Of course she did. And the rest is history. They've been together for more than twenty years.

All because my mom is the ultimate romantic.

Given the popularity of rom-coms, romance novels,[1] and pop songs about true love and broken hearts, we're clearly just as much in love with love as ever. But despite the general popularity of romance, love stories are often treated as unserious and frivolous—and feminine. Harlequin romances and other novels that make love the central plot element are considered "chick-lit"—they're given pink cover art (sometimes with glitter, often with shoes, lipstick, or shopping bags) and persistently ignored by highbrow book lists. Love songs get the same treatment—when performed by women. How many times has Taylor Swift been lambasted for "only" writing songs about her relationships? Ditto romantic movies and soap operas and Hallmark Hall of Fame TV movies. If it's about love, we tell ourselves as a culture, it's not serious, and it's really just for girls.

Jennifer Weiner to *Vogue* on why she spoke out about the unfair treatment of women's commercial fiction: "It was, 'This isn't fair and I'm going to say something about it.' Of course, some of it was personal. Obviously, who wouldn't love to get that giant *New York Times* review? But some of it was, 'You review mysteries and you review science fiction and you review Stephen King but yet the entire genre of romance, which is by far the most popular and the most profitable, you won't touch that.' What does that say about all those women readers? Why are they not important enough to deserve visibility?"

We even sometimes characterize love stories as dangerous. A primary criticism of fairy tales is that they seem to advance the idea that the only worthy goal for girls and women is falling in love, which could dissuade them from pursuing other aims. To be a romantic, in other words, is not just to be frivolous but to be pathetically distracted by love.

It's powerful to be a romantic because romance is an expression of life's richness; it attends passion and courts poetry. It invites enchantment, intrigue, adventure, influence, fascination, charm, devotion, and delight. It makes magic out of the mundane and recognizes the infinite sparkling worth in our day-to-day. It can shape our moments and our impressions, and that is power.

—Amy Rosenthal, creative director, Model10Electra

DID YOU KNOW? One of the long-standing critiques of fairy tales—especially the modern, commercial versions of the traditional stories—is that in making love a goal, they send a message that women's highest aim should be love. The original stories, of course, came from a time when love for love's sake was a radical idea (and when any other path to a different life for women was unthinkable)—which is worth thinking about. But the stories themselves reach far beyond that: the goal in those stories isn't just love, it's freedom. Cinderella, Snow White, the Little Mermaid—they're all good-hearted, feminine characters, but the core plot of each of their stories centers on their determination to decide their own paths. Striving to move away from abusive homes or toward new worlds of discovery, each of these characters seeks to make a better, more interesting, more empowered future for herself. Each is driven by the desire to decide for herself what she wants her life to be and to pursue that. Which is what we all want, right? To choose whom we will love, where we will live, and the family, friends, and community we will have. And if that involves getting to wear the most beautiful glass footwear imaginable, that's just a bonus.

Why is the belief in and pursuit of love considered a bad thing? It is, of course, possible to overvalue romance. Focusing on it to the exclusion of other goals and values isn't healthy or productive; love doesn't (despite the oft-misinterpreted axiom) conquer all, and so looking to love to solve bigger problems, for example, can be a futile and sometimes dangerous exercise (think of the abused wife who believes that her love can change her spouse).

Books, films, music, and TV have always shaped cultural ideas of romance that are, yes, sometimes unrealistic (the archetypal love story, *Romeo and Juliet*, will never be praised for its realism). These stories about courtship, love, sex, marriage, and family are literally romanticized, and for many they become the gold standard for what relationships should look like. They feed our fantasies and imaginations. "It's clear that media and film can shape and reinforce prevailing cultural attitudes," says Dr. Silvia Kratzer, professor of cinema studies at the University of California at Los Angeles's Department of Theater, Film, and Television. "Real changes in people's lives because of pop culture influences are evident—just think of the beauty ideals that have changed so much."

I'm a hopeless romantic. It's disgusting. It really is. I've seen While You Were Sleeping, *like, twenty times, and I still believe in the whole Prince Charming thing.*

—Jennifer Love Hewitt, actress

I'm a hopeless romantic. I buy things because I fall in love with them. I never buy anything just because it's valuable.

—Iris Apfel, businesswoman, interior designer, and fashion icon

The downside of this, of course, is the chance that we won't
accept real life when it doesn't measure up to the dreamy realities presented on the big screen or in the pages of a book. That's
informed how we think of the so-called hopeless romantic: the
person (most often a girl or woman) who yearns for the fairytale
versions of love and life. We do think of that person as, if not
truly hopeless, then to some extent helpless, having subjected
herself to idealized goals. But what if we reframe "hopeless" as
"hopeful"? Being a romantic is partially about seeing the world
in the best possible light. It's about believing in the power of
human connection and the force of the heart. Shouldn't looking at things through rose-colored glasses result in a more
beautiful and connected world? Because romance and love are
not just about sex and coupling. Love is about the connected
power of the human heart and spirit and transcends physical
relationships.

So, while holding up love as the only worthy goal in life
might certainly be problematic (for both women and men),
outright rejecting love as a worthy goal feels shortsighted—and
even disempowering. So does rejecting faith in love and an aspiration to find it—because loving and being loved are crucial
to a good life for individuals, families, and communities, and
loving well requires that we value love. We need to believe in
the power of love if we are to use it meaningfully. How could
it be otherwise?

Loving relationships make us feel good. Love inspires and
motivates us. Romantic connection is the foundation for the
long-term relationships that yield security and children. Relationship and connection are the cornerstones of community—
love, as the songwriters say, will keep us together—and of
human thriving. Love lifts us up where we belong. If faith and
belief in that is a feminine thing, let's claim it—because it's a
powerful thing.

HOW TO BE ROMANTIC

Watch rom-coms and read love stories. True, our lives will never look exactly like the ones we see on the big screen. But if those movies and TV shows inspire us to believe in magic and keep on going, that's great! If those movies put a smile on your face, watch more of them.

Write love letters. To your lover, your spouse, your best friend—anyone who touches your heart.

Make romantic gestures whenever you can—to yourself and others. Buy flowers for yourself or your loved ones. Put a rosebud in a vase on the dinner table. Light candles. Say I love you. Say it again.

Do you understand we're right now in the midst of the women's revolution. Right now, we're in women's liberation. Before, we were fighting to be men. That's not being a woman.

—PAT ALLEN, PhD

CHAPTER 21

LOVE FULLY

The best and most beautiful things in this world cannot be seen or even heard, but must be felt with the heart.

—HELEN KELLER, AUTHOR

The stereotype of women as consumed by or obsessed with love is well established and long-standing. We are characterized as loving too easily or too enthusiastically or too intensely; we get described as "lovesick" or "love starved." We are told that we love too much, that we're too giving and too generous in love, and that we do much in vain to make relationships work. There are endless books, memes, movies, and songs on the subject of women's tendency to love too fully. We're the desperate Heloise, the besotted Juliet, the heartbroken Anna Karenina tossing herself in front of a train. The trope of the heartsick young woman sobbing about a boy into a carton of ice cream is only the most contemporary manifestation of this idea.

The behaviors associated with the stereotype of the lovesick woman are, of course, often frowned upon—and in some cases with good reason. Staying too long in bad relationships and pining over unavailable men aren't great things. And "loving too much" in general can be draining and generally unhealthy. We may shut down. We may decide it's easier to be single. We may hold back our love. We may cultivate resentments toward the loved ones who aren't loving us in the way that we want. And on top of it all, we risk being perceived as weak. We're likely to be judged for the very feelings we're having about ourselves (e.g., he's never going to commit, but she stays with him anyway).

We believe, however, that loving fully carries far more rewards than risks. As we discussed in Chapter 1 on being emotional, our emotions are powerful and can be a source of power. Love is one of our most powerful emotions and so can be one of the greatest sources of personal power—and a force for much greater good. We are deeply emotional beings, and love is our currency.

AMY'S STORY

I met an extraordinary man two years ago, and we had one of the most magical, romantic days of my life. I was attending a three-day summit of 3,000 entrepreneurs, business leaders, social impact pioneers, and change makers—on a cruise ship in the Bahamas. This man and I were both up early on the last day and started it with an interpretive dance class to no music on the top deck of the ship. The day unfolded with adventure and fun—everything from the water slides and ropes course on the ship, to a swim at a local beach and a visit to the best lobster shack on the island of Nassau, to long talks in several Jacuzzis on the boat, all ending with The Wailers and a big dance party. He and I connected on multiple levels (physically, emotionally, and intellectually), and because of where and when we met, we were both completely in the moment and present. It was a day I'll never forget. It wasn't clear if we'd ever see each other again—he lived in Europe and had no plans to be back in the United States.

We stayed in touch. We happened to be in Ibiza at the same time the following summer and spent another spectacular eighteen hours together. He had been threatening to come to Los Angeles (even said he might want to live here). When he finally planned a trip to LA in the summer of 2017 and his plans fell through, he invited me to join him in Sri Lanka. Even though I had spent a total of (less than) forty-eight hours with this man, my response was an unequivocal yes. A month later, I was on my way. (Honestly, I wasn't even sure exactly where Sri Lanka was until after I booked the trip!) Friends thought I was crazy to go on a ten-day trip with a guy I barely knew.

Somehow, even in our brief time together, I knew we would have a wonderful time. And I was right. Our trip was adventurous, free, romantic, challenging, unexpected, intense, and relaxed. It was like a honeymoon, topped off with a rose petal bath and champagne on our final night together.

And then we both went back to our respective homes. It was done. I was crushed. I cried the whole way home (and it's a *long* way home). We had experienced such a wide range of things and emotions over those ten days. I opened myself up, showed myself, let myself fall. I felt so close to him, so attached. Of course, I wished there were a way we could be together (the romantic in me believed that where there's a will, there's a way). That said, we aren't in the same place in life: he is focused on work and happy to be living freely; I am focused on creating a more balanced life and opening up space for love, ready to settle down. It seems men are sometimes better at compartmentalizing; he was, at least.

A few of my close friends have asked the same question: Was it worth it? My answer has always been a resounding yes. What an incredible moment we shared. I'm so grateful to have connected so deeply with this man.

I grew and learned so much from the experience and practiced opening up, letting go, and loving fully, regardless of the potential outcome. I chose love. And I will continue to choose love.

She was ready to deny the existence of space and time rather than admit that love might not be eternal.

—SIMONE DE BEAUVOIR, THE MANDARINS

A long tradition of philosophic thought recognizes love—and sometimes the feminine propensity to love—as a crucial force in both individual and social human development. The power of love in general has been examined as far back as Plato, whose *Symposium* examines love as a philosophical concept and as essential to human well-being. Jean-Jacques Rousseau argued that an education in love was crucial to the development of good citizens and that women, and mothers in particular, naturally provided this education because of their inclination to love openly. Sometimes, of course, this idea has taken unfortunate (sexist) turns: Rousseau also said that women were unfit teachers in any other capacity because their love for their children—so valuable in teaching affection—would prevent them from being unbiased. He also believed that it complicated their citizenship: they would, he said, be unable to put country before family. Others argued that women's tendency to love too much made them unsuitable for philosophy: women are (the argument goes) less likely than men to put love of wisdom before romantic or familial love. And, of course, most of us are familiar with the theological idea that women are too attached to spouse and family to love God or a church as fully as men. Still, philosophy, theology, art, and literature agree that love is an unequivocal good, and women are important purveyors of (certain kinds of) love.

You don't need a humanities degree to grasp the underlying truth here. Love is a wonderful thing and crucial to human flourishing. And it doesn't matter whether we look at the capacity to love fully as an inherently feminine characteristic—loving fully is good, full stop. Sure, there are extremes to avoid, but that holds for anything.

When we're feeling good and in the positive flow of our emotions, we're more inclined to be loving. It's easy to love in those times. When we're *not* feeling so good, we are more inclined to keep to ourselves, put up our armor, and share less. Loving fully means that even when we're not feeling particularly loving, we still choose love over the alternative. We don't let fear get in the way or worry about the implications: that we might not be loved back or loved as much or that we might ultimately be rejected. We love fully because it feels better—under all circumstances.

And we love fully because it frees us of the negative. It allows us to lean fully into our best, most loving selves. We leave fear behind, knowing that love is a more powerful and productive force than fear. And choosing love over fear—fear of rejection, of heartbreak, of disappointment—is powerful in and of itself. Choosing love demonstrates our personal capacity for love and fuels the human capacity for love. When we love fully, we make it possible for others to love fully—again and again and across all circumstances. Imagine a world in which we all loved fully.

Here's the bottom line: When we hold back, we only hurt ourselves. When we love fully, we give more love and experience more love. Seems like an easy choice.

We are most powerful when we love with our whole hearts. So, let's do more of that.

USING THE POWER OF LOVE

Resist fear. Use painful or challenging moments as training. The next time your fear or insecurity is triggered and you find yourself pulling back, do the opposite: lean in. If you feel someone pulling away or are uncomfortable with an interaction with a friend or colleague, approach the situation with love. What happens when you consciously choose love over fear?

Accept the worst-case scenario. Imagine that things (at work, in a relationship, etc.) don't work out as you would hope. Imagine things going down the toilet. Will you be OK? (Spoiler: the answer is yes.) Now that you've resolved that, won't the whole experience, regardless of the outcome, be better and happier if you're in a loving state? (The answer is also yes.)

Make love a daily practice. Think about how you move throughout your day: How can you bring more love into it?

Maybe it's by writing a thoughtful note to a friend, volunteering at a soup kitchen, fostering kittens, or committing to a daily practice of expressing your love to loved ones. And don't forget self-love: How are you taking care of yourself? What's the loving choice for *you* in any moment?

Remember that love can be bigger than you. Love can be a form of resistance; it can be a revolution. Author Glennon Doyle Melton coined the term "love warrior," and it's a good one. She insists that love is, in fact, a weapon, but a positive one. Make love a part of your politics. If more of us did that, we'd change the world.

We're in the middle of a revolution right now, a movement that we won't even understand how big until years down the road.

—CAT CORA, WORLD-RENOWNED CHEF, AUTHOR, AND RESTAURATEUR

CONCLUSION

There seems to be a rediscovering by women of the divine feminine presence within them, a remembering that from the dawn of mankind, it's always been the fundamental differences between them and men that hold their greatest power. These women know that innate female qualities such as intuition, compassion, nurturing, peacemaking, healing, and teaching are not weak characteristics, but incredibly powerful and absolutely essential to a world suffering from too much self-interest and aggression.

—Dr. Habib Sadeghi,
cofounder of Be Hive of Healing

So, where do we go from here?

We've shared twenty-one practices of feminine power. And they are just that—practices—meaning they only really unlock power to the extent that you use them regularly. Make whichever ones spark for you habits, even—*especially*—those that feel contradictory. Take control and let go. Be good and be wild. Dream big and take action. Take care of others and let yourself be taken care of. Be mysterious and be open; lean in and lean back; be your glorious, complex, powerful feminine self.

You are woman. You don't just contain contradictions, you embrace them. You celebrate them. So, go ahead: find yours and make them sing.

Be emotional. Your emotions are your power. Wear them proudly.

Cry openly. Reveal yourself to loved ones without holding back.

Allow yourself to mother those around you at home, at work, wherever you feel like a little nurturing will go a long way.

Be chatty. Communicate and build community and connection with those around you.

Unleash the full power of your intuition and trust it. Use your witchy ways.

Be expressive! Don't hold back! Share your joy!

Unleash your sexual power. Find freedom through your sensuality.

Flirt freely and widely. Enjoy your feminine charm.

Allow yourself to dream. Imagine what's possible and follow your heart.

Surrender. Let go. Find freedom through this release.

Don't underestimate the power of being agreeable. The world needs a little more politeness, kindness, and grace.

Do apologize. Build bridges and create deeper connections.

Be glamorous. Express yourself through style and approach.

Own your weakness. Be vulnerable. Allow others to support you.

Be seductive. Use your power to create intrigue and connection.

Be your wild and womanly self. Lose control. Don't hold back.

Be controlling. Exercise your magnificent organizational skills. Be the boss that you are.

Lead from behind—or beside. Embrace opportunities to be a deputy or an ally, an advisor or supporter. Discover the power of playing a supporting role.

Sing and dance. Express your creative self freely and beautifully.

Be romantic. Imagine and create beauty. See the world through rose-colored glasses.

Love fully. Let your heart lead you.

Again, some of these principles will spark more naturally for you than others. Others may not spark for you at all. What matters is this: that as you join us on this feminine journey, you explore as many and as much of them as you can. Play with them! Experiment. See what resonates for you, both in your day-to-day experience and in the bigger picture.

We think that this represents a new way of living and fully expressing our feminine selves. A softer, gentler, and more connected way to live, relate, and experience the world and each other. A more observant, intuitive, emotionally oriented, and loving way of being. It liberates us from cultural stereotypes and socially imposed constraints. It gives us the freedom—and encourages us—to live as the best possible versions of ourselves.

At the same time leaning into our femininity isn't always going to be easy. We all have deeply ingrained habits and established patterns—many of which inhibit our feminine powers. They may be tough to let go of—and some you may not want to let go of at all. That's fine. The beauty of this is, you get to choose. You get to define what femininity looks like for you.

For the tough stuff that you do want to tackle, we've provided plenty of tools and ideas, and we hope that you'll turn those to your own use. And remember, this isn't meant to be work; it's meant to be exploration. There's no right or wrong way. It's only what you want it to be—and whatever that is, give it room to be messy. You might find yourself celebrating your amazing feminine powers of staying in control and then, all of the sudden, flipping out at the office or on your kid and thinking, "Uh oh, I'm not doing this as well as I thought." That's when you go back to the chapter on losing control and remind yourself that there's power in that too! The bottom line: don't be so hard on yourself.

of that description that could have any correlation with the word "weak." They're all strengths. But for some reason, we've been socialized to look at those qualities as weak qualities. As less than. So I think that that's something that we have clear up, and most of the heavy lifting is on us men. In order to find balance and to live in a world where there is real parity, equality, and equity, a big part of it has to be men being okay with themselves while also being willing to learn from women, who naturally embody more of those feminine qualities and who have also been socialized to express them.

—JUSTIN BALDONI, ACTOR

And as you put these principles into practice, encourage those around you to do the same. This is a feminine sisterhood. As we allow ourselves to more fully express these parts of ourselves, we have an opportunity to model and celebrate this for the women around us: our mothers, daughters, sisters, coworkers, employees, bosses, and friends. Think about how you can create the space for the women in your world to be part of this new feminine experience.

And men, of course, are a crucial part of this conversation too. When we tap into our feminine power, men and boys benefit too. Not just because it allows us to deepen our relationships with everyone in our world, but because it opens a world of feminine possibility for men too. We've spent millennia adopting their values, behaviors, and postures. What happens if we invite them to celebrate ours? Femininity and masculinity need each other—but in balance. Showing the men and boys in our lives how extraordinarily powerful femininity is opens up the possibility of real, meaningful harmony between femininity and masculinity.

And we need that—for our relationships and for our world. We need a world in which love is as celebrated as strength and where compassion is as desirable as control. We need a world in which girls who want to be president or CEO know that they can bring their caring, feeling selves to that stage and that those qualities only enhance their intelligence and capacity for leadership. And we need a world in which men respect and elevate the power of femininity—for our sakes and for theirs. We want boys and men, as well as girls and women, to recognize that mothers do hard, important work—and that the work involved in nurturing and protecting home and family is hard, important work no matter who does it. We want girls to be proud to love princesses—and boys to be proud to love princesses too. We want girls and women to know that they can love crafts and baking *and* be rocket scientists or CEOs. We want to be sexy, and we want to be secure. We want to love and be loved fully.

I feel that where people lose their sense of what femininity is, is when they try to cater to what men think it is. It almost feels like we need a new word. Femininity, there's been so much negative attached to it that there's this understanding that femininity is not an external thing, it's only a positive thing, and it should be embraced and all that. I feel like in order for society to 100 percent go along with it, we need a new word or something.

—JORDYN WIEBER, OLYMPIC GYMNAST

I love my femininity, it's who I am. I embrace it. I'm still a badass motherfucker.

—CHRISTINE SIMMONS, PRESIDENT AND COO, LA SPARKS

And we really do think that's possible. We think getting there starts with conversations like this one.

So, let's keep opening this up. Let's keep talking about the bigger issues around how men and women can thrive together. Let's keep opening up space for men to find balance between their masculine and feminine qualities and ways of being. Let's make this a priority in how we talk to our children. Imagine if we invited and encouraged girls and boys to explore these issues from a young age. Imagine how this would help with understanding and opening up a two-way dialog.

Through this conversation, we happen to open up the opportunity for a happier, more connected, more balanced world. It starts with us.

It all starts with you.

Remember, strength through grace.

xo Amy and Catherine

The things that are happening in the world right now fighting against the patriarchal norms that women have been forced to comply with for centuries. . . . These things are—hopefully— becoming a thing of the past. For us, as women, to perceive ourselves or who we are—the innate qualities we possess—in any negative light only gives life to those limited, antiquated views.

—SELA WARD, ACTRESS

ABOUT THE AUTHORS

With a background in traditional marketing and deep experience in marketing to and building brands for women, Amy Stanton has a unique perspective on the women's landscape, the role of femininity in personal and professional lives, and the impact that unleashing our true feminine power can have on happiness.

Amy founded Stanton & Company (S&Co) with a passion for promoting and building positive female role models and messaging for women. Since 2006, when the company opened its doors, S&Co has built a roster of philosophy-driven brands, including exceptional athletes, lifestyle experts, and brands in the healthy, active living space.

Before founding Stanton & Company, Amy served as the first-ever chief marketing officer (CMO) for Martha Stewart Living Omnimedia and was the head of marketing and communications for NYC2012, New York's Olympic bid, where she developed and executed both the local and international campaigns for this first-ever endeavor. Amy started her career in account management at advertising agencies including BBDO, JWT, and BBH.

Between her leadership roles on Fortune 500 accounts in advertising, her role as the CMO at Martha Stewart Living Omnimedia, and, most recently, as founder and CEO of an twelve-year-strong marketing and PR agency focused on building female-focused brands, Amy has deep experience in the women's space and a wide range of relationships with powerful women who have inspired her thinking about femininity and how women can be their best. Amy has received accolades and awards from the *Sports Business Journal* and Women in Sports and Events (WISE) LA, and Stanton & Company has been recognized as an industry leader. She speaks about marketing and representation, women in sports, and women's leadership.

Catherine Connors (MA, PhD/ABD; University of Toronto) combines an academic background as a social theory scholar with extensive professional experience in women's media. As an academic, she spent years studying the place of women and girls in social and political thought and the influence of ideas about femininity on ancient, modern, and contemporary society. As editor in chief of *Babble* and head of content for Disney Interactive's Women and Family portfolio, she oversaw the publication of hundreds of thousands of stories about women's lives, reaching over 40 million readers, and developed a rich understanding of the audience for such stories and of their dreams, ambitions, anxieties, and fears. Catherine's personal site, Her Bad Mother, has similarly reached an audience of millions of (mostly) women since its debut over a decade ago and has been featured in, among many others, the *New York Times*, the *Washington Post*, the *Globe and Mail*, the *Toronto Star*, the *American Prospect*, and the *London Times*, as well as on CNN, ABC, CBC, and BBC Online. Catherine is an in-demand speaker and has been a featured commentator on most major media outlets, including CNN, NPR, and *Good Morning America*, addressing a variety of topics related to women's lifestyle, feminism, parenting, and family life. Catherine is also the cofounder and chief creative officer of Maverick, a creative network for girls and young women.

NOTES

CHAPTER 2: CRY OPENLY

1. See Bylsma, Journal of Research in Personality, 2011.

2. William H. Frey, *Crying: The Mystery of Tears* (Minneapolis: Winston Press, 1985).

CHAPTER 4: BE CHATTY

1. Julie Huynh, "Study Finds No Difference in the Amount Men and Women Talk," Undergraduate Biology Research Program, University of Arizona, June 19, 2014, https://ubrp.arizona.edu/study-finds-no-difference -in-the-amount-men-and-women-talk; Claudia Hammond, "Prattle of the Sexes: Do Women Talk More Than Men?," BBC, November 12, 2013, http://www.bbc.com/future/story/20131112-do-women-talk-more-than -men; Jeff Guo, "Researchers Have Found a Major Problem with 'The Little Mermaid' and Other Disney Movies," Wonkblog (blog), *Washington Post*, January 25, 2016, https://www.washingtonpost.com/news/wonk /wp/2016/01/25/researchers-have-discovered-a-major-problem-with-the -little-mermaid-and-other-disney-movies.

2. Deborah Jones, "Gossip: Notes on Women's Oral Culture," in *The Feminist Critique of Language: A Reader*, ed. Deborah Cameron, 242–251 (London: Routledge, 1990).

3. Deborah Tannen, *You Just Don't Understand: Women and Men in Conversation* (New York: HarperCollins, 1991), 77.

CHAPTER 5: OWN YOUR INTUITION

1. Scholar Nelly Richard, in *Masculine/Feminine: Practices of Difference* (Durham, NC: Duke University Press, 2004), notes that the inherent masculinity of the dominant knowledge system doesn't—or shouldn't—"impede women from taking it over by storm" (14).

2. See, for example, W. Ickes, *Everyday Mindreading: Understanding What People Think and Feel* (Amherst, NY: Prometheus, 2003); D. G. Myers, *Intuition: Its Powers and Perils* (New Haven, CT: Yale University Press, 2002).

CHAPTER 8: FLIRT FREELY

1. David Dryden Henningsen, "Flirting with Meaning: An Examination of Miscommunication in Flirting Interactions," *Sex Roles* 50, nos. 7–8 (April 2004): 481–489.

CHAPTER 10: SURRENDER

1. Holger Afflerbach and Hew Strachan, *How Fighting Ends: A History of Surrender* (Oxford: Oxford University Press, 2012).

CHAPTER 16: UNLEASH YOUR WILD WOMAN

1. Raj Raghunathan, "Why Losing Control Can Make You Happier," *Greater Good Magazine*, September 28, 2016, https://greatergood .berkeley.edu/article/item/why_losing_control_make_you_happier.

CHAPTER 17: BE CONTROLLING

1. Leslie Bradshaw, "The Sheryl Sandberg Effect: Rise of Female COOs," NPR, August 9, 2013, https://www.npr.org/sections /alltechconsidered/2013/08/06/209483329/the-sheryl-sandberg -effect-rise-of-female-coos.

2. Bradshaw, "The Sheryl Sandberg Effect."

CHAPTER 20: BE ROMANTIC

1. There are 75 million readers of romance novels.

THE FEMININE REVOLUTION
READING LIST

A Return to Love, Marianne Williamson
Are You There God? It's Me, Margaret, Judy Blume
Bad Feminist, Roxane Gay
Cinderella Ate My Daughter, Peggy Orenstein
*Daring Greatly: How the Courage to Be Vulnerable Transforms the Way We
      Live, Love, Parent, and Lead*, Brené Brown
Delusions of Gender, Cordelia Fine
Femininity, Susan Brownmiller
feminism is for everybody, bell hooks
Fortytude, Sarah Brokaw
Gender Trouble, Judith Butler
Getting to I Do, Dr. Pat Allen
Girlfighting, Lyn Mikel Brown
He's a Stud, She's a Slut, Jessica Valenti
Heart Talk, Cleo Wade
How to Be Parisian Wherever You Are, Anne Berest, Audrey Diwan,
      Caroline de Maigret, and Sophie Mas
Intuitive Being, Jill Willard
Lean In, Sheryl Sandberg
Love Her Wild, Atticus
Love Warrior, Glennon Doyle Melton
Meeting at the Crossroads, Carol Gilligan and Lyn Mikel Brown
Mom & Me & Mom, Maya Angelou

Moody Bitches, Julie Holland, MD

My Foot Is Too Big for the Glass Slipper, Gabby Reece

On Female Body Experience, Iris Marion Young

Redefining Realness: My Path to Womanhood, Identity, Love and So Much More, Janet Mock

Sense and Sensibility, Jane Austen

The Beauty Myth, Naomi Wolf

The Book of the City of Ladies, Christine de Pizan

The Chalice and the Blade, Riane Eisler

The Feminine in Fairy Tales, Marie-Louise von Franz

The Feminine Mystique, Betty Friedan

The Joy Luck Club, Amy Tan

The Mermaid and the Minotaur, Diane Dinnerstein

The Myth of the Nice Girl, Fran Hauser

The Old Wives Fairy Tale Book, Angela Carter

The She Book, Tanya Markul

The Surrender Experiment, Michael Singer

The Uterus Is a Feature, Not a Bug, Sarah Lacy

The Way of the Superior Man, David Deida

Too Fat, Too Slutty, Too Loud: The Rise and Reign of Unruly Women, Cordelia Fine

Vagina, Naomi Wolf

We Should All Be Feminists, Chimimanda Ngozi Adichie

We Were Feminists Once, Andi Zeisler

We: A Manifesto for Women Everywhere, Gillian Anderson and Jennifer Nadel

Woman Hollering Creek, Sandra Cisneros

Women Who Run with the Wolves, Clarissa Pinkola Estés

ACKNOWLEDGMENTS

First and foremost, we would like to thank the many spectacular women (and men) who were interviewed for *The Feminine Revolution*. These include Paula Abdul, Dr. Pat Allen, Jamie Anderson, Liz Arch, Chloe and Halle Bailey, Courtney Bailey, Ilyse Baker, Justin Baldoni, Tiffany Bartolacci, Liz Bentley, Sara Bordo, Karen Brodkin, Sarah Brokaw, Jodi Guber Brufsky, Dawn Cartwright, Kristen Castree, Cari Champion, Cat Cora, Cindy Crawford, Deborah Curtis, Shelia Darcey, Jenna Elfman, Nicole Ehrlich, Julie Foudy, Jennifer Carroll Foy, Courtney Nichols Gould, Emily Greener, Jennifer Grey, Jan Stanton Holz, Alexis Jones, Elise Loehnen, Geeta Novotny, Malia Mills, Nikki Monninger, Melissa Palmer, Shel Pink, Amy Powell, Michele Promaulayko, Gabby Reece, Daunnette Reyome, Amy Ilyse Rosenthal, Dr. Habib Sadeghi, Christine Simmons, Ellen Taylor, Sela Ward, Jordyn Wieber, Marianne Williamson, Jill Willard, and Shelley Zalis. We are also so deeply grateful for Jimmy Pitaro, who introduced the two of us originally.

AMY

This book is the result of inspiration, thinking, and support from so many people in my life, and I'm deeply grateful to each and every one.

First and foremost, thank you to Catherine, who, aside from being a brilliant mind, has been a committed, passionate, and kind partner throughout this process.

Thank you to our wonderful literary agent, Coleen O'Shea, with whom I've worked on many projects and now I can finally claim her as mine—her guidance and passion have been invaluable. Thank you to Laura Mazer and our excellent team at Seal Press—we knew from our first conversation with you that this was the right home for *The Feminine Revolution* and are grateful for the partnership.

I am surrounded by the most incredible friends and family and am grateful for constant love, support, enthusiasm, and inspiration—it wouldn't be fun doing any of this without all of you. My S&Co girls are my extended family—thank you for your love and support, for keeping me on my toes, and for your ongoing dedication and hard work, making it possible for me to pursue this creative project. Dr. Sadeghi, thank you for your love and mentorship and for helping me integrate the spirituality and power of femininity in my own life. Thank you to my sweet Bernard—you are my sunshine.

And finally, my biggest thanks to my rock, my first and most consistent feminine role model, my mom. She has shown me from day one that anything is possible.

CATHERINE

They say that it takes a village to raise a child. I have never tested that theory with actual children, so I can't speak to its truth as a statement on child-rearing, but I can say that it does apply to writing and publishing a book. So many people were a part of the "raising" of this work, and I am indebted to each and every one of them.

First thanks, of course, go to Amy, from whose wonderful mind the idea for this book was born, and who continually inspired me and challenged me to think harder and better about the ideas we were exploring. And to our literary agent, Coleen, and our brilliant editor, Laura: thank you both for being such caring stewards of this work.

To my team at Maverick: this book was conceived in the early days of the project that became Maverick, and many of the ideas within it were shaped and refined as Maverick itself was shaped and refined. This would not be the work that it is without that influence—and yours.

To my nephew Tanner, who passed away just before this book went to press: sweet boy, you were and will always be, for me, the greatest example of how kindness, gentleness, and sensitivity transcend gender. And you proved, unquestionably, that love is a superpower. Thank you.

To my mom, and to my dad: your love, encouragement, and inspiration made me the woman that I am, and there will never be enough thanks for that.

To my daughter, Emilia, and my son, Jasper: thank you for teaching me that princesses can be badasses, dirtbikes go with sequins, imagination is a superpower, and that girls and boys alike are made of sugar, spice, and everything awesome.

And finally, to my husband Kyle: thank you. I could not have done this without you. I love you.